The Book of Jonah

Insights for the Christian Faith

Dr. Tony L. Warrick

A Theological Commentary

For information about special discounts available for bulk purchases, sales promotions, fundraising and educational- or theological needs, contact Dr. Tony L. Warrick at TonyWarrick.com.

The information presented in this book is presented for educational purposes only. The commentary and other contents reflect the opinions of Dr. Tony L. Warrick and are based on his studentship and research.

Cover design by Jamar Jones, www.gi-designs.com

Editorial services by Nyesha Sherman and Maryanne Dingman

Printed in the United States of America

Visit the author's website at www.TonyWarrick.com.

ISBN: 978-1-955253-01-7

Before We Get Started

Before we get started, if something is troubling your heart and robbing you of your peace of mind, I urge you to allow me and my team to pray for you. Send me a prayer request so my team and I can join you in prayer:

tonywarrick.com/prayerrequest/

Also, don't forget to subscribe to my website and catch all my new releases, daily devotionals, and monthly newsletter. You can sign up here: **tonywarrick.com**

Table of Contents

Dedication

Dear Heavenly Father,

I dedicate this book to You, the Most-High God. May this book be used to pass on the promise of hope, forgiveness, life, and community. May this book help the readers remember those who are forgotten – the hungry, the lonely, the homeless, the vulnerable – yet are significant citizens in Your kingdom of Heaven.

This book is my offering to You, with the faith and confidence that all I say, all I think, and all I hope will take root in this world and be the source of new expressions of Your love, Your justice, Your character, Your grace and of Your reign through Jesus Christ, our King.

May Your will be done on earth as it is in Heaven, in Jesus' name, I pray, Amen.

Introduction

I do not know if you realized it or not, but we run a lot. We run home, we run to the store, we run away for the weekend, we run with an idea, and there are times we run to the bathroom. Nevertheless, our most dangerous running happens when we run from situations, trials, and issues.

Take a good look at your life. Is there anything that you are running from right now? Are you running from your work? Your responsibilities?

Are you running from your relationships? Your singlehood, if you are single? Your deteriorating health? Your poor dietary habits?

Maybe you are running from your inadequate exercise regime? Your negative financial status? Your goals? Your aspirations? Your family and your past?

We have seen individuals who mentally and emotionally run to avoid obstacles, challenges, and problems in life. However, I have learned that if you don't face your issues, no matter what you are trying to run from, avoid or dodge, difficulties and problems will ultimately seep into your fears, surround your sorrows, and eventually rest upon your dissatisfactions.

In relationships, escapism materializes when individuals rebound after painful breakups. Rather than deal with the situation, they avoid their sadness and seek comfort in someone else. The thought and feeling of being desired and wanted by someone cover up the pain of their breakup; it covers up the pain of being lonely. And while the person may seem to have escaped dealing with the pain head-on, in reality, this trauma has not been adequately addressed nor healed. It is just there, dormant, throbbing silently until the day when it resurfaces differently, creating chaos, fear, anger, insecurity, and confusion.

I have seen people run from things in other areas of life as well—for example, socially shy people who run from public appearances. I know individuals who are afraid of failure, so they run from their passions by finding comfort and security in passionless jobs. I have met people who want to be loved but run from love because they are scared others will reject them for being themselves. I have counseled individuals who avoid their past because their past reminds them of their deepest afflictions.

If I'm honest, I have met individuals who spend their whole lives running from God because they are scared their friends and family will reject them. I've even seen people run from God because they believe there will be repercussions for their past. They think they are not worthy, nor will they receive God's love, mercy, and grace. Here is my question for you:

Are you running from your God?

We all know that sometimes those who believe in the Lord run from the Lord. Why? Every so often, God asks us to do things we do not want to do, even though He is only looking out for our best interest and the interest of His people. Sometimes, those things He asks us to do are painful; sometimes, those tasks are uncomfortable.

So, I will ask you another question: Are you like Jonah, running from God's will for your life?

The book of Jonah has a wealth of knowledge to offer on the mere surface level about running from the will of God. However, it desires to teach us a more profound lesson that we are not able to perceive without assistance. Sometimes a lesson is waiting to be learned just below the surface of the text if we will take the time to unearth it. After all, it is the glory of God to conceal a matter, but the glory of kings to search it out (Proverbs 25:2).

In the book of Jonah, you will discover that Jonah did not want to obey God. Therefore, he ran in the opposite direction only to find out that he could not outrun the Father. Challenges chased Jonah down, including a giant fish that swallowed him whole. It was only in this terrifying ordeal that Jonah cried out to the Lord for help.

How often do you do the same thing?

Do you ignore God until misfortune strikes?

Do you cry out for help when you feel like the pain is too unbearable?

God is so gracious and merciful that when Jonah cried out for help, He did not hesitate. In the depths of his hopelessness, Jonah called out to God, and our heavenly Father gave him another chance to right his wrong.

When we run from God, things often become more complex. We hit more roadblocks, suffer more problems, and become more frustrated. But if we follow God's lead, He can guide us to a promised land of purpose, fulfillment, and prosperity. We may have to make sacrifices as we strive to do the right thing, but it is through the right way, God's way, that He rains down His blessings.

The story of Jonah is one of the clearest demonstrations of God's love and mercy for all humanity. This book, ***Jonah: Insights for the Christian Faith***, seeks to provide understanding into what God is teaching through the book of Jonah. By analyzing and expounding, chapter by chapter and verse by verse, this theological commentary will examine the complete biblical story.

Even though Jonah's story is only four short chapters, it is filled with valuable lessons. Lessons like:

- how to obey God when He asks you to do something you don't want to do.
- how to love people who act and look different than you.
- how God's grace can change the heart of someone you're sure won't change.
- how we become blind to our own need for grace.

But most importantly, we can learn that God is more loving, gracious, and in control than we can imagine.

Vital Information

Before we take a deep dive into the book of Jonah, let's look at some vital information

Authorship

According to tradition, this book is thought to have been written by Jonah, the son of Amittai. Jonah is a prophet of the northern kingdom of Israel in about the 8th century B.C.

The biblical book of Jonah is different from other prophetic books because it focuses on the prophet's actions and does not focus on his prophecies. As a matter of fact, only one verse summarizes his message to the people of Nineveh.

Historical Background

According to 2 Kings 14:25, Jonah ministered during the time of Jeroboam II. During this time, Jeroboam was expanding the borders of his kingdom. This expansion was made possible by a decline and failure in Assyrian supremacy. Along with Jonah, God sent the prophets Hosea and Amos to inform Israel of imminent judgment. Israel's failure to repent and return to God brought about this judgment through Sargon II and the Assyrian attack in 722 B.C.

Date

The events recorded in this book, in all probability, covered only a few weeks at the most. Jonah lived during Jeroboam II's reign over the Northern Kingdom of Israel (789 - 748 B.C.). Based on studentship and research, I can assert that Jonah probably wrote this book sometime between 785 – 775 B.C.

Original Audience

Jonah was writing to all the people of Israel. Today, the book of Jonah is read on Yom Kippur, the Day of Atonement, which is considered one of the most important holidays in the Jewish faith.

Original Purpose

The book of Jonah is written to demonstrate the extent of God's sovereign power, love, and grace for Israel by His decision to withhold His judgment from the people of Nineveh, a gentile nation.

Overall Theme

God's compassion and mercy await us no matter our past behavior if we only repent full-heartedly.

Key Verses

Jonah 2:9 - "But I with the voice of thanksgiving will sacrifice to you; what I have vowed I will pay. Salvation belongs to the Lord!"

Jonah 4:11 - "And should not I pity Nineveh, that great city, in which there are more than 120,000 persons who do not know their right hand from their left, and also much cattle?"

Validation

Most modern scholars deny the historicity of the book of Jonah and consider it to be an allegory. The story's miraculous elements are chief reasons for this, particularly the great fish swallowing the prophet and the vine's rapid growth. Hence, many scholars argue that the author never intended the reader to understand the account as historical. Jonah's blatant disobedience, miraculous deliverance, the conversion of an enemy city of Israel, and the prophet's pouting have led some to conclude that this is a fictitious satire.

However, there are four reasons why I reject these arguments:

1. Jonah is identified as a historical person in other books of the Bible.
2. Nineveh was a historic city.

3. God's relationship to the prophet is presented as historical.
4. The Messiah, Jesus, referred to Jonah's experience with the great fish as well as the repentance of the city of Nineveh as historical realities.

Notes on the Commentary

Many of my comments are drawn from the insights of Jewish and Christian theologians. My insights into the book of Jonah have been gleaned from classic Jewish interpretations and early Christian thought. Nonetheless, since my perspective is through the lens of Jesus the Messiah and his Apostles, my insights, understanding, and application may take a different approach to the text. I will often use traditional Jewish interpretations as a springboard for additional insights that are pertinent to Christians. This commentary aims to turn to the wisdom of those who had gone before us and handed down both interpretation and tradition that have withstood the test of time.

Chapter 1

Jonah Disobeys

First Commission of Jonah

Jonah 1:1

"Now the word of the LORD came to Jonah the son of Amittai, saying,"

When God calls, what is the proper response? It seems impossible to say no to the Lord's commands, so unimaginable that running away takes the place of words. So, who is this Jonah who ran when God called?

Jewish tradition identified Jonah as a member of the Company of Prophets mentioned in connection with Elisha's ministry (2 Kings 2:3). He was the prophet who Elisha commissioned to anoint Jehu (2 Kings 9:1–10). In addition, scripture identifies him as bringing God's Word to Jeroboam II, king of Israel (2 Kings 14:25). This is where Jonah predicts that Jeroboam will recover certain lost territories.

Jonah's original Hebrew name is *"Yonah."* Yonah means "dove," which is the same word used in Noah's story in Genesis 8. The name Amittai derives from the Hebrew word *"emet,"* which means "truth." We need to understand that the recording of the name of a significant individual's father was standard in

Hebrew writings, and the existence of Amittai's name in the text authenticates the historical reality of Jonah.

According to the Talmud (the basic compendium of Jewish law and thought), Jonah's wife used to join him on his pilgrimage to Jerusalem three times a year during the festivals to become more connected to God. It is taught that Jonah's wife recognized her husband's shortcomings in his efforts to become closer to the Lord. So, by willingly joining the pilgrimage, Jonah's wife served as an example for her husband to constantly strive to become closer to God's will.

Jonah's hometown was Gath-hepher, a border village in ancient Israel (2 Kings 14:25), located about three miles northeast of Nazareth, Jesus' hometown. The etymology of the name Gath-hepher means "wine-press of the digging."

Note: According to the Mishnah (a book of rabbinic interpretations of the Hebrew Bible), Jonah's mother was of the tribe of Asher and his father of the tribe of Zebulun. Furthermore, Jewish tradition mentions that Jonah is the son of the "woman of Zarephath." If that statement is true, then Jonah may be the one whom Elijah revived from the dead. (1 Kings 17:21–23).

The Value of a Good Name

If we are honest, we know Jonah's name is associated with two specific things. It is associated with a big fish and disobedience. But have you ever thought about what is associated with your name? Does your name define who you are and what others perceive about you? What does it mean to have a good name?

Shakespeare was right to ask what's in a name because names matter. Actually, every time you hear a name, you make several assumptions about that individual, business, or product. A name categorizes you, but it does so much more.

Our names are a part of our public persona. To a certain degree, our names tell people who we are, what we do, and a little about how we do it. Truthfully, when we see a name, we draw conclusions about various characteristics – age, class, and race. A person's name implies their worth, character, authority, and reputation.

If you were to ask people on the street to list what matters the most in their lives, you would probably hear things such as family, God, career, wealth, and many other commonly shared values. However, I do not think you would hear many claims about the importance of "a good name." But a good name is significant and valuable.

A good name is one's reputation, an honorable reputation. Proverbs 22:1 says, ***"A good name is to be chosen rather than great riches…",*** but how many times have we overlooked that truth? If one has a famous name, that person is treated with reverence and honor. If they have a name associated with ill-repute, disrespect and ridicule will follow. A good name, a good reputation is worth preserving and protecting.

Never underestimate the value of your name. Your good name will bring you the favor of others. Your good name provides stability. Your good name is theoretically eternal.

You need to live in such a way that if someone speaks unkindly about you, no one would believe it. Always remember, the blessing that comes with a good name will not only last a lifetime but often will be remembered long after one has left this world.

Jonah 1:2

"Arise, go to Nineveh, that great city, and call out against it, for their evil has come up before me."

Question: Have you ever wondered why God would send Jonah to deliver a message to the inhabitants of a non-Israelite city?

According to the Bible, God did not send any other prophet to speak to a non-Israelite city or town. All the other biblical prophets were sent to preach to the people of Judah or Israel. Furthermore, Nineveh is not just any non-Israelite city; it is the Assyrian empire's capital, known for its cruelty to Israel and Judah.

In Genesis 10:8-12, we can see that Nineveh's history stretched back as far as Nimrod, who built it, as well as Babel, and many other cities in Mesopotamia. Nineveh occupied about 1800 acres and stood on the east bank of the Tigris River. The ancient fort of Nineveh was situated on a hill, and on that hill, there were also Assyrian royal palaces and temples. Within the first 50 years of its establishment, Nineveh would become the Assyrian empire's capital.

Note: Ninevah's ruins are across the river from the modern-day major city of Mosul in Iraq, 500 miles northeast of Israel.

In verse two, the phrase "call out against it" means notifying the people that the God of Israel had noticed their wickedness. The book of Jonah does not explain the wickedness that has drawn God's attention to Nineveh. However, the prophet Nahum gives us more insight into their sinful ways.

Nahum says that Nineveh was guilty of wicked plots against God, exploiting the helpless, cruelty in war, and practicing idolatry, prostitution, and witchcraft (Nahum 1:9-3:4). We can learn from this verse that God takes notice of the sins of the world when their evil grows in violence and inhospitableness.

The Inconvenience of Serving God

Have you ever thought about how inconvenient it could have been for Jonah to go to Nineveh? Think about it: He probably had his day planned. Jonah probably knew what was supposed to happen that week. He probably knew who he was supposed to talk to, who he was supposed to see, and what tasks he was supposed to accomplish. But then, boom, the Lord's instructions come and what he had planned to do just doesn't get done.

We have our daily routines. With work, bible study, family time, and church on Sundays, we frequently forget that God does not operate according to our schedule. Every now and then, God will allow us to serve Him and glorify Him at times that interfere with our day. Nevertheless, how we respond to this inconvenience reflects where our heart stands with God's will for our lives.

We need to understand that our time and resources are not ours! This means that everything belongs to God. Our heavenly Father is the creator and owner of all things, and He has only given each of us a portion of His abundance to manage while we are here on this earth. We are called to be good stewards.

"As each has received a gift, use it to serve one another, as good stewards of God's varied grace: whoever speaks, as one who speaks oracles of God; whoever serves, as one who serves by the strength that God supplies—in order that in everything God may be glorified through Jesus Christ. To him belong glory and dominion forever and ever. Amen" (1 Peter 4:10-11).

Now, if everything you have is a gift from God, and He gives it to you for a while to steward, you need to understand that you get the joy of both receiving and providing the abundance He possesses. Therefore, with everything you have and with all of who you are, start seeing your inconvenience as an opportunity to serve God and others. Knowing who is the source of all things shows us how to use all things.

Lastly, one of the keys to releasing God's supernatural power in your life is serving the Lord and others. Don't miss an opportunity to be a part of what God is doing; it is so much fun!

Jonah 1:3

"But Jonah rose to flee to Tarshish from the presence of the Lord. He went down to Joppa and found a ship going to Tarshish. So he paid the fare and went down into it, to go with them to Tarshish, away from the presence of the Lord."

Why does Jonah run away? Why does Jonah reject God's call to go to Nineveh? How could a prophet respond to God's call in such a disrespectful way? The apparent explanation is that he fled because he was terrified of what would happen to him. He was worried that if he went to Nineveh, the Ninevites would torture and then execute him.

Another obvious explanation is that Jonah had grown to hate the Assyrians. His hatred was so intense that he didn't want God to save them and show compassion toward them. He was upset that God expressed concerns for the non-Israelite Ninevites. Jonah is unwilling to offer God's forgiveness to such people.

If we look beyond the obvious reasons, Jonah has placed the honor of the people of Israel over God's goodness. He portrays himself as a hero sacrificing himself for the benefit of the people of Israel. In other words, Jonah understood that God had a specific job for him. Still, he didn't want to do it, so Jonah chose disobedience over obedience.

Jonah headed west to a port called Tarshish. It is most likely impossible to locate the exact spot that Jonah planned to visit. However, Tarshish was a port in which silver, iron, tin, lead, ivory, monkeys, and peacocks were traded. It was about 2,500 miles west from Joppa, and Joppa stood about 35 miles southwest of Samaria, the Northern Kingdom of Israel's capital. Nineveh lay about 550 miles northeast of Samaria.

Note: Today, Joppa is called Jaffa, and it is an ancient port city in Israel. Jaffa is located in the southern and oldest part of Tel Aviv.

Have you ever wondered why Jonah fled to the sea? Jonah could have hidden in a cave in the mountains, but he ran towards the sea. Why?

According to Talmudic sages, the Land of Israel is higher than all other lands. This is not meant in a geographical sense; instead, it means that the Holy Land is the most suitable place to relate and connect to God and the primary location to engage in the observance of God's commandments. In other words, when one moves to Israel, it is said that one is elevating themselves, and when one leaves the Land of Israel, it is said that one has descended.

In the Bible, encounters with God often take place on the mountaintops.

- God instructs Abraham to offer Isaac as a sacrifice on Mount Moriah (Genesis 22:2).
- God appears to Moses in the burning bush on a mountain (Exodus 3:1).
- God gives Moses the Torah on Mount Sinai (Exodus 19:20).
- Solomon builds the Temple in Jerusalem, which is called the Temple Mount (1 Kings 6:1).
- Elijah confronts the prophets of Ba'al on Mount Carmel (1 Kings 18:20).

Therefore, when Jonah "went down" to the port, and then he "went down" to the ship, and "went down" into the hold of the ship, he could have thought by descending and fleeing to the sea, he would escape God's providence and presence.

As we will see throughout this book, Jonah's theological beliefs become a persistent obstruction in his ability to become God's faithful servant.

The following map shows Jonah's journey.

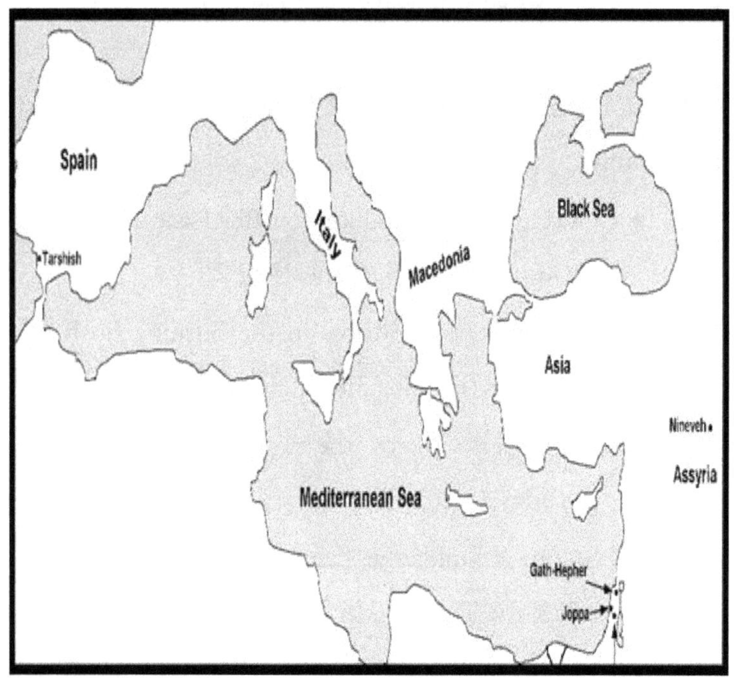

Running from God's Calling

When we don't understand God's will or simply don't like it, we're often tempted to do things our own way. Have you seen how children hide from their parents when they are about to be disobedient? We do the same thing and try to hide from the presence of the Lord when we don't accept His will for our lives.

There will be seasons in your life where you're comfortable; seasons where you're enjoying the favor and blessings of God. However, the Lord is not going to leave you in your comfortable place all the time. Why? Because there is an assignment on your life. A mission only you can complete.

Can I be honest with you? There was a time in my life where I felt like Jonah. And like Jonah, I ran away from my God-given mandate, thinking that would solve my problems, and I would not have to face my fears.

However, I learned three valuable lessons:

1. When you run away from God, innocent individuals, including those you care about, can get hurt because of your disobedience.
2. The calling on your life is not about you. It's about the people directly and indirectly attached to your obedience.
3. If you make people the focus, you will find out that it's you who benefits most.

Always remember, you have an extraordinary calling on your life, and God wants you to fulfill that calling. You may be tempted to quit or run away from the difficulty. But understand that you cannot reach new levels without being uncomfortable and stepping outside your comfort zone.

God may call you to make changes in your friendships. He may call you to step out and start a business. He may ask you to leave the familiar and go into the unknown. But when God gives you an assignment, He grants you the grace and strength to complete the assignment at hand.

God has equipped you with His grace to finish what He has designed and destined for you. Therefore, go where He says go. Stay where He says stay. Do what the Lord says to do.

You can obey God's calling on your life confidently and quickly because His ways will always bring life, purpose, peace, and provision – in His time and His way. Never forget Ephesians 4:1-3, ***"I therefore, a prisoner for the Lord, urge you to walk in a manner worthy of the calling to which you have been called, with all humility and gentleness, with patience, bearing with one another in love, eager to maintain the unity of the Spirit in the bond of peace."***

Jonah 1:4-6

"But the Lord hurled a great wind upon the sea, and there was a mighty tempest on the sea, so that the ship threatened to break up. Then the sailors were afraid, and each cried out to his god. And they hurled the cargo that was in the ship into the sea to lighten it for them. But Jonah had gone down into the inner part of the ship and had lain down and was fast asleep.

So the captain came and said to him, "What do you mean, you sleeper? Arise, call out to your god! Perhaps the god will give a thought to us, that we may not perish."

The sea to ancient Israel was the essence of disordered forces that humans could not control or tame. Therefore, it is essential to understand that the great wind upon the sea was not just to bring about the storm but also to keep those on the ship from reaching dry land. We can also conclude that God sent the wind to blow in a specific direction because we know that the sailors were unable to bring the ship closer to the shore, which means that the storm came from the direction of land toward the open sea.

The ship Jonah boarded was probably a large trading vessel with a deck, and the sailors were of diverse religious beliefs. In their fear of the great wind, the text shows us that the sailors cried out and called each to his god. This approach grows out of the belief that such a severe storm must be an act of a deity in response to a human being's misdeeds.

Let's look closer to the phrase in verse 5, "each cried out to his god."

In the singular, the phrasing shows that the sailors did not share a common god. According to several Jewish historians, every nationality of idolater was represented on the ship. If that is true, the ship then becomes a microcosm for the entire gentile world.

Throughout rabbinic literature, we find the concept that the world contains 70 nations. This idea grows out of the list of the 70 male descendants of Noah (Genesis 10:1-29). Knowing this, if the ship included every nation's representative, the ship had a crew of 70 sailors, which means prayers of 70 sailors to 70 different gods produced no results.

The sailors' willingness to throw their cargo into the sea shows the life-threatening danger they faced. On the contrast, Jonah's ability to sleep under such conditions seems very unusual and odd. While the sailors cried to their gods, Jonah did not cry out to the Lord. Why? Was Jonah's sleepiness a sign of carelessness, or was it a sign of something more profound?

Psychologists tell us that some people who suffer from misery, depression, or fear of something happening choose to sleep to escape. This may be what Jonah was doing. Maybe, he was going to sleep to escape the chaos, to escape the pain he felt. Perhaps, for Jonah, he slept, but he preferred death.

The captain of the ship concluded that the prayers of the sailors wouldn't stop the storm. He saw Jonah's prayers as their last hope, even though he did not know if the God of Jonah would be greater than all the gods of the sailors. The captain finds Jonah hiding in the ship's hold, hoping that maybe Jonah's prayers will be his salvation.

Note: In Mark 4: 35-41, we read how Jesus Christ calms a storm. One of the reasons the disciples were filled with great fear was because, like their forefathers, they believed the sea was the essence of chaotic forces, and no one could control or tame it. The symbolism behind the story of Jesus calming the storm should bring great encouragement and hope for anyone facing a storm in life.

God is in Charge of the Storm

Most of the time, we believe God is in control and in charge when everything is going our way. When everything is going great, we declare that God's will is being done. When life is good, the family is pleased, business is thriving, and sales are up, we know God is directing our steps. However, having faith in the Lord during great days does not exempt us from difficulties, nor does problems mean a lack of His blessings and sovereignty in our lives.

The storm is an instrument of God's grace. On the surface, it seems like God is punishing Jonah. But when we look closely, God is helping Jonah realize his transgression. God is getting Jonah's attention through the storm. Question: Does the Lord need to send a storm to get your attention?

The storms of life come to every person. It rains on the just and unjust. When the mighty wind blows, it impacts the righteous and the wicked. When the waves of life crash down, it doesn't matter if we are corrupt or honest, we all have to swim, or we will drown. In fact, Jesus once said, ***"In the world, you will have tribulation" (John 16:33).***

In difficult times, it's easy to think, "God, where are you? How could you let this happen to me?" But the same God in control and in charge during the good times is just as in control and in charge during the tough times. God will not allow a storm to come into our lives unless He has a divine purpose for it, even when we don't understand.

Here's the key: When the storms of life come to test and challenge your faith, you can take hope in the fact that God is your anchor, keeping you steady even when chaos swirls around you.

God will direct the winds of the storm to blow you where He wants you to go. You may see storms as unfavorable, but God uses storms to move you from point A to point B. The winds may be strong, the conditions may look bleak, but if you stay in faith and not get bitter or start complaining, those winds will shift you into your destiny.

Are storms scary? Yes! But please understand that all sunshine and no rain make a desert. In other words, too much of one thing can hurt you.

Therefore, consider it a gift when you encounter trials, for the testing of your faith produces unwavering strength, hope, and inner peace.

Results of Disobedience

Jonah 1:7

"And they said to one another, "Come, let us cast lots, that we may know on whose account this evil has come upon us." So they cast lots, and the lot fell on Jonah."

After throwing their cargo overboard to lighten the ship and realizing that their prayers and outcries did not improve their situation, they relied on other methods to prove that the storm was not natural but instead, the result of divine influence. However, something is interesting about this event. Weren't there other ships in the sea? And is it standard practice for sailors in a storm at sea to cast lots to learn whose account for the evil which fell on them?

According to Pirke de-Rabbi Eliezer (a non-legalistic exegesis on Hebrew stories), chapter 10, the great storm Jonah and the sailors encountered was not an ordinary storm. Ships to their left and right were passing back and forth in peace. The vessel that Jonah had boarded was in great trouble and was about to be destroyed. If this is true, it will offer context to why the sailors said, "Come, let us cast lots, that we may know on whose account this evil has come upon us."

The sailors' confidence in the random act of casting lots seems absurd to us. Nevertheless, it appears to have been a common practice among the nations to help decide or determine who was accountable for some calamity. Furthermore, casting lots was a prescribed method of learning God's will in Israel. Ancient Israelites believed that if they prayed before casting lots, then God would guide them in their choice.

For modern readers of the Bible, there is limited access to understanding what exactly lots were. Some scholars suggest lots could be sticks with markings, stones with symbols, or some kind of dice, thrown into a small area and then interpreted. The primary reason for casting lots was to render an impartial, unbiased decision on essential matters. Once the lot was cast, no one could argue that the decision resulted from human intervention like nepotism, politics, favoritism, and so on.

In the Bible, the practice of casting lots was used in a variety of circumstances, including:

- The selection of the scapegoat (Leviticus 16:8–10).
- The distribution of the tribal inheritance in the Promised Land (Numbers 26:55, 56; Joshua 14:2).

- The determination of the families who had to relocate to give a proper distribution of the populace (Nehemiah 11:1).
- The order of the priests and their duties (1 Chronicles 24:5–19; Nehemiah 10:34).
- The determination of an offender (Joshua 7:14–18; Proverbs 18:18).

In the New Testament, after Judas killed himself, the disciples cast lots to see who would be his replacement (Acts 1:12–26). After the day of Pentecost, the Bible does not have any instance of Believers casting lots to discern the will of God; therefore, I conclude that after the arrival of the Holy Spirit, we do not need to rely on casting lots but instead must rely on our relationship with God through the ministry of His Holy Spirit.

Note: The practice of casting lots is mentioned more than 70 times in the Old Testament and at least seven times in the New Testament. Despite the many references to casting lots in the Old Testament, nothing is known about the actual lots themselves in the book of Jonah. The closest modern practice to casting lots is likely flipping a coin.

Did you notice that the author, Jonah, said, "they cast lots," in the plural? This plural form means the sailor did not cast lots only once but multiple times. If they had cast lots only one time, the fact that it fell on Jonah might have been the result of random chance. Instead, they cast lots several times, and changed the lots, but each time the lot fell on Jonah and not his shipmates. In this case, God intervened and gave the sailors the correct answer to their request.

Jonah 1:8-9

Then they said to him, "Tell us on whose account this evil has come upon us. What is your occupation? And where do you come from? What is your country? And of what people are you?" And he said to them, "I am a Hebrew, and I fear the LORD, the God of heaven, who made the sea and the dry land."

The sailors did not immediately seize Jonah, and they did not immediately throw him into the sea. Instead, they did an additional investigation and interrogated him when they believed they had identified the guilty individual responsible for their calamity. They wanted to understand what transgression Jonah had committed so they could make an informed decision. These sailors were not only men of action but also men of self-examination.

Theodor Gaster offers this insight into the sailors' questions:

> "It is a common superstition that it is dangerous to sail with an impious or wicked person since his presence aboard will inevitably provoke an outraged god to embroil the sea and possibly wreak the ship."

Regardless of whether Theodor Gaster's insight is correct or not, we know the sailors seemed sure that their unwarranted position was because of Jonah.

When Jonah says to them, "I am a Hebrew," they would have known about his people and land. But why does Jonah declare himself to be a Hebrew and not a Jew? The term "Hebrew" is the name by which the Israelites' neighbors knew them. Furthermore, in Jonah's time, the term "Jew" was not yet used to describe a member of the nation of Israel.

If you ask twenty-first century Jews who were the first Jews, they will quickly tell you Abraham and Sarah. However, Abraham and Sarah would not have recognized the term Jew because it derives from the name of one of their grandsons, Judah, and the tribe that descended from him.

The tribe of Judah was the dominant group in the Southern Kingdom during the First Temple period. Following the destruction of the Northern Kingdom and its ten tribes, the tribe of Judah becomes the dominant group in the nation. During the Second Temple period, the country is called Judea. Late Hebrew Bible books, which include the New Testament books, use the term Jew. Therefore, in the context of the time and place in which Jonah lived, it is natural for Jonah to identify himself as a Hebrew.

Lastly, it was vital for Jonah to identify himself as a Hebrew because it explained that he worshiped the God of Israel, the creator of Heaven and earth, the creator of the sea and land. The fact that they believe Jonah's God made the sea on which they traveled, as well as the dry land, convinced the sailors that Jonah had done something severe. Previously, the sailors had feared the storm, but now they feared the Lord, recognizing the Creator above the creation.

Note: In the ancient Middle East, the true test of a god's power and authority was if he could control the sea. Hence, in Luke 8:25, the disciples of Jesus were afraid and marveled at Jesus' ability to command the storm.

Who Are You?

As the sailors learned about the identity of Jonah, let me ask you one of the most illuminating questions you can ask someone: Who are you?

As you can imagine, the question by itself can be superficial. Even so, take your time and think about it.

Did you identify yourself by occupation, family lineage, or achieved endeavors? Did you answer the question by identifying yourself by your associations and affiliations? Did you identify yourself by your given name or where you were born?

Who or what are you allowing to determine your identity? Are you seeing yourself correctly?

For many of us, our identities center on our accomplishments, heritage, talents, skills, jobs, children, our past, or marital status. We can also find many of our identities wrapped in some form of trauma, poverty, or failure. However, that is not who we are!

If you are going to be everything God created you to be, you have to stop letting people and situations define who you really are. It does not matter if it's your parents, spouse, girlfriend or boyfriend, boss, or even your friends; you must stop allowing individuals to put you into their mold. Therefore, instead of letting people define you, and letting your past label you, focus on what God says about you. He is the one that created you.

You must accept these never-failing truths:

- You are the visible expression of the invisible God, who takes delight in seeing His excellent plan for your life unfold.
- You are a member of a chosen race, a royal priesthood, a holy nation, anointed by God.
- You are not mediocre; you're unique, fearfully and wonderfully made.

Remind yourself that you are strong, you are courageous, you are capable, and you are equipped to fulfill your dreams and manifest your destiny. God has made you powerful, an overcomer, and a winner, which means you are victorious.

Who are you?

You are a child of the Most-High God! A citizen of the Kingdom of God, an Ambassador for Christ with diplomatic immunity.

Jonah 1:10-12

Then the men were exceedingly afraid and said to him, "What is this that you have done!" For the men knew that he was fleeing from the presence of the LORD, because he had told them. Then they said to him, "What shall we do to you, that the sea may quiet down for us?" For the sea grew more and more tempestuous. He said to them, "Pick me up and hurl me into the sea; then the sea will quiet down for you, for I know it is because of me that this great tempest has come upon you."

The sailors realized the cause of their great difficulty in this journey; therefore, they asked Jonah another question: What is this that you have done? This question was not just a question; instead, it was an expression as if to say, how could you have done such an evil thing to flee from the presence of the Lord who created the sea and land?

The sailors might have known what to do with Jonah if he was a criminal or convicted of some wrongdoing. But, Jonah was guilty of being a runaway servant of his God and directly disobeying His orders. The sailors were puzzled! They had no idea how to calm the Creator of the sea, so they asked Jonah for guidance since he knew his God best.

Still, Jonah was not ready to obey God, and he was not ready to repent and continue his life as a prophet. Nevertheless, his sympathy for the sailors led him to give them a plan designed to release them from God's reprimand. However, it would also result in Jonah's death, which he regarded as more desirable than obeying the Lord. His heart was still as hard as ever toward the Ninevites even though he acknowledged that he knew God was disciplining him.

Can Bad Things Be Good?

Let's pause for a moment and step in the shoes of the sailors in this story. Most of these sailors were minding their business, trying to get from point A to point B. Then a mighty storm comes threatening to kill them. Truth be told, they are victims of unfortunate circumstances.

If we, as Christians, were in a similar situation as the sailors, one of the very first things we would do is blame the Devil. However, the Devil didn't have anything to do with the sailors' unfortunate situation, which makes me wonder if the Devil is involved in your unfortunate circumstances. Is it possible that you are having problems because someone in your life is disobedient to the Lord? But I digress.

If we are honest, we frequently find ourselves the victims of unfortunate circumstances, whether through other people's hands, calamity, natural disasters, complicated situations, or even poor choices. Nothing may be going our way, and we may feel that all the cards are stacked against us. We can overcome this victim mentality by understanding that, although we may have our own plans for our lives, our lives are not our own, and they ultimately belong in the hands of the Lord.

"The heart of man plans his way, but the Lord establishes his steps (Proverbs 16:9)."

Joseph understood this principle well (Genesis 45:5-8) and gave credit to God even for the circumstances in his life that most individuals would consider horrifying. Joseph understood that the Lord was the one who was in control and in charge of his affairs. Later, he reminded his brothers, ***"As for you, you meant evil against me, but God meant it for good, to bring it about that many people should be kept alive, as they are today" (Genesis 50:20).***

Understanding this principle is not an easy task. We all struggle in some way and push back against God's divine will. Nonetheless, we have two decisions. We can either blame others and become victims or trust that our Creator has our best interest at heart.

Please always remember that you may not be able to change your circumstances, but you can change your attitude. And changing your attitude can often change your circumstances. Changing your attitude allows your God to show Himself faithful. So, can bad things be good? Absolutely, it can! If we allow the Lord to have His way.

Jonah 1:13-16

"Nevertheless, the men rowed hard to get back to dry land, but they could not, for the sea grew more and more tempestuous against them. Therefore they called out to the LORD, "O LORD, let us not perish for this man's life, and lay not on us innocent blood, for you, O LORD, have done as it pleased you." So they picked up Jonah and hurled him into the sea, and the sea ceased from its raging. Then the men feared the LORD exceedingly, and they offered a sacrifice to the LORD and made vows."

Man overboard!

To save the ship and its sailors, Jonah was cast into the raging sea. As far as the sailors are concerned, Jonah has died, the sea is miraculously calm, and the unbelievable ordeal is over. If this were to be the end, Jonah would be remembered as the prophet who refused to obey God and paid the price for it. However, in God's plan, this is not the end of the story.

The sailors initially rejected Jonah's advice because they could not accept the truth that Jonah had shared with them. They did not want to believe that the only way to save their lives is to take his life by throwing him into the sea. They did not want Jonah's blood on their hands. Instead, they rowed and exerted themselves to get back to the shore.

The sailors believed that they could use their skills to overcome the storm and save Jonah. However, God, the Creator of the heavens and earth, did not choose this path for Jonah, for He wanted Jonah, of his own free will, to repent and obey His original command to preach to Nineveh. Therefore, the storm became more severe against the ship, preventing the sailors from overcoming the conditions created by God.

When reaching land became impossible due to the ferocious sea, they prayed to the God of Israel and voiced their belief in His authority over the storm. The sailors did not want to be punished based on what they were about to do to Jonah. They wanted to be sure that everyone on the ship understood their actions were fulfilling Jonah's wishes and not an act of violence.

The text shows us Jonah's entering the sea was the reason why the storm stopped raging. However, I would like to draw your attention to exactly how the sailors threw Jonah into the sea. According to Pirke de Rabbi Eliezer:

> They took him (and cast him into the sea) up to his knee-joints, and the sea-storm abated. They took him up again to themselves, and the sea became agitated again against them. They cast him in

> (again) up to his neck, and the sea-storm abated. Once more, they lifted him up in their midst, and the sea was again agitated against them until they cast him in entirely, and immediately the sea-storm abated.

According to the Jewish Sages, they lowered Jonah into the sea and pulled him out to see the truth of the matter. After they pulled him out of the sea several times, the sailors finally lowered Jonah into the sea to stay.

We can now conclude that the sailors did not rush to judgment; they did not rely on the casting of lots, nor did they take Jonah at his word when he told them what they had to do. They attempted a less radical approach, and they tried to row to shore. And even when they begin to accept that they need to cast Jonah into the sea to save the ship and themselves, they proceed slowly.

Verse 16 tells us that the sailors offered sacrifices to the God of Israel. However, it does not tell us when, how, or the kind of vows the sailors made. These sailors were most likely polytheists, so we should not conclude that they abandoned their worship of other gods. This means they did not convert to the God of Israel but merely acknowledged that the God of

Heaven, who made the sea and the dry land, caused the storm and spared their lives.

Our God is Greater

Polytheism is the worship or belief in multiple deities usually assembled into a pantheon of gods and goddesses, along with their religions and rituals. But did you know the term "god" was a generic term? The word "god" is derived from the Proto-Germanic word *"gudán,"* which means ruler. Hence is the reason why the Lord teaches us that we shall have no other gods (rulers) before Him.

"You shall have no other gods before me (Exodus 20:3).

So, what are these "other gods"? They are anything or anyone that we worship and assign ultimate authority and influence to. For example, did you know that kings and pharaohs are called gods or sons of gods in the Bible? They are called gods or sons of gods because of their authority, power, and influence.

In its origins, polytheism was not devised in opposition to monotheism but as a flawed effort to better serve the one true God. Early civilizations believed by giving honor to the various forces of nature that God had set in place, they were showing honor to their Creator. Over time, this transferred into complete adoration of these forces, giving them independent authority and becoming gods. In other words, early societies started worshipping the creation rather than the Creator. They started giving honor to kings instead of giving honor to the King.

We need to understand individuals put in power positions and the forces of nature have no power of their own and are entirely dependent upon God, "like a wrench in the hands of a mechanic." While the mechanic's inspired creativity and capacity may be channeled through the tool, the tool has no power of its own. As Daniel wisely said, ***"He changes times and seasons; he removes kings and sets up kings; he gives wisdom to the wise and knowledge to those who have understanding" (Daniel 2:21).***

When we acknowledge that God is greater than anyone or anything, it changes our whole perspective about the Lord's rights and sovereignty. We find ourselves submitting to Him and trusting Him to do what's best. Though we may not understand why He allows what He does in this world, we rest in the confidence that He triumphs over all in the end. We don't have to understand everything to trust Him. He is GOD, the Holy One of Israel, the One of whom there is none greater!

The Lord created you to lean on Him, to depend on Him. He is on your side and worthy of your trust. If we cling to God, He will hold us and guide us to live our best life for Him. In order to do so, we have to seek Him daily, remain in prayer, and remind ourselves what the Bible says about giving God control.

Now, my question to you is: who is the ruler of your life?

Jonah 1:17

"And the LORD appointed a great fish to swallow up Jonah. And Jonah was in the belly of the fish three days and three nights."

Did you know that the great fish is only revealed in the text three times in the book of Jonah? Yet, it dominates the thinking of people who are quick to dismiss its theological legitimacy. The fish is not the main character. It plays a tiny part, a supporting role, in conjunction with all of the other conduits of nature that God sent to Jonah to force self-confrontation. In other words, the individuals who pay too much attention to the fish's existence in this story miss the meaning of the story in an attempt to disprove its historicity.

The type of great fish remains a mystery since the only record of this fish is in this story. The Hebrew word *"dag,"* translated as "fish," describes an assortment of aquatic creatures. Many people believe Jonah was in the belly of a whale, even though the original Hebrew translation does not confirm it was a whale. However, we can ensure that God saved Jonah's life by using a big fish rather than a more predictable method such as providing previously tossed cargo or a piece of wood that he could hang on to for survival.

This verse shows us that Jonah being swallowed by the great fish was not a divine act of divine punishment but divine preservation. The great fish was both a sanctuary and a conveyer for Jonah.

According to Rabbi Tarfon, the great fish that swallowed Jonah had been assigned this task since the fifth day of Creation (Genesis 1:20-22). He continued by saying,

> The Lord provided a huge fish to swallow Jonah. Jonah entered its mouth the way a man enters a large synagogue. He stood there, and the eyes of the fish shone down upon him like two skylights.

Rabbi Tarfon implies that the miracle of the fish's arrival is connected to the miracle of the fish's very design so that Jonah would instantly know that this fish was sent to him by God as an act of love rather than a punishment.

Nonetheless, for Jonah to proclaim the God of Israel and call out against the people of Nineveh, a nation that didn't have a relationship with God, his message would have had to captivate his listeners and make a cultural and social impact. It is probably for this reason that God chose to save Jonah by using a great fish. The incident would have shown the Ninevites that the God of Israel can control the traditionally uncontrollable, revealing His great authority and His gracious heart.

Jonah's deliverance was significant because it became a type and shadow of an even more significant event that took three days. Jesus Christ cited Jonah's experience to illustrate the Messiah's death and resurrection (Matthew 12:40–41). The death and resurrection of Jesus would captivate his listeners and make a cultural and social impact.

Chapter 2

Jonah Repents

Jonah's Prayer

Jonah 2:1

"Then Jonah prayed to the LORD his God from the belly of the fish,"

When Jonah first arrives in the belly of the fish, does he believe that he will be saved, or does he think he will die?

The text does not offer an answer, and the book of Jonah does not tell us when, during the three days, Jonah begins to pray. However, I believe initially, Jonah is not sure how to comprehend the situation. And some time during day two or three, when Jonah realizes he wasn't going to die, he started to believe that salvation is his. Therefore, he prayed to God.

Additionally, I believe Jonah could have composed most of this prayer while he was inside the great fish and gracefully completed and polished the prayer sometime after he was safely on dry land. In the original manuscript, Jonah speaks in the past tense throughout the prayer. The prayer is a single piece, and the ideas flow without interruption from verse to verse, describing his descent, repentance, and devotion to the Lord who saves him.

The text tells us that Jonah directs his prayer "to the Lord his God." Why does Jonah include both "the Lord" and "his God"? It is because "the Lord" addresses God's authority, who is the Supreme Ruler, and "his God" addresses his relationship with the Supreme Ruler. Jonah recognizes that being alive in the belly of the fish is not an accident but a step in the right direction toward his salvation.

Start with Prayer

Reading about Jonah being swallowed by a great fish makes me wonder if you have ever felt swallowed up by life? Have you felt consumed by hopelessness, struggle, fear, or guilt? Have you ever felt broken? I hope you're not feeling that way at this very moment, but if you do, start with prayer.

When you are confronted with a hopeless situation and feel overwhelmed, you need to look up to God in prayer because prayer is an indispensable spiritual weapon. In fact, prayer is the greatest of all forces because it honors God and brings Him into active aid. Prayer will focus your attention on the Lord and help you see that He is greater and more powerful than any of your concerns and circumstances. Prayer is where our deficiency meets God's sufficiency.

It's not just about a one-time prayer, either. Some problems are so deeply rooted that only persistent prayer will solve them. If you genuinely want to see something happen in your life, pray about it over and over. Regardless of what things look like in the natural, never give up on prayer; stay devoted to it.

"Rejoice always, pray without ceasing, give thanks in all circumstances; for this is the will of God in Christ Jesus for you" (1 Thessalonians 5:16-18).

To overcome what you are going through, you will have to rise above it with prayer because a small prayer can change your life in a big way. And please never forget, it was an act of prayer that finally moved Jonah from a prophet drifting to a prophet with newfound direction, with a renewed commitment to becoming the trailblazer God expected him to be. Prayer is not the last resort; it is the first step.

Jonah 2:2-9

he said,

"I called out to the LORD, out of my distress, and he answered me; out of the belly of Sheol I cried, and you heard my voice. For you cast me into the deep, into the heart of the seas, and the flood surrounded me; all your waves and your billows passed over me. Then I said, I am driven away from your sight; yet I shall again look upon your holy temple.

The waters closed in over me to take my life; the deep surrounded me; weeds were wrapped about my head at the roots of the mountains. I went down to the land whose bars closed upon me forever; yet you brought up my life from the pit, O LORD my God.

When my life was fainting away, I remembered the LORD, and my prayer came to you, into your holy temple. Those who pay regard to vain idols forsake their hope of steadfast love. But I with the voice of thanksgiving will sacrifice to you; what I have vowed I will pay. Salvation belongs to the LORD!"

While Jonah was in the belly of the fish, he was praying a prayer of thanksgiving and not a prayer of deliverance. He was thankful that he had not drowned because drowning was a particularly distasteful form of death in the ancient Near East. Jonah's ability to thank God during tribulation shows that he experienced a noteworthy change in attitude and mindset. He changed from a fugitive on the run into a prophet prepared to fulfill his calling.

Many of the concepts in Jonah's prayer are from the book of Psalms and are rooted in a well-known prayer language. Clearly, he knew the psalms well, and he could have spent much time reflecting on them during his three days in the fish. The following table will show how his prayer is rooted in the book of Psalms.

Jonah's Prayer	**The book of Psalms**
2:2 - I called out to the LORD, out of my distress, and he answered me	**120:1** - In my distress, I called to the Lord, and he answered me.
2:3 - all your waves and your billows passed over me.	**42:7** - all your breakers and your waves have gone over me.
2:4 - I am driven away from your sight.	**31:22** - I am cut off from your sight.

Pray Specifically

We can learn a lot from Jonah's example of prayer in chapter 2. Such as, when we know what's causing our hopelessness, we should pray specific prayers for what we need.

I have prayed to God my entire life, but I have not always prayed specifically. Why? Because, to a certain degree, praying specifically exposes my vulnerability. It is similar to when a friend asks how you are doing, and you don't reveal the whole truth because you are trying to hold back heartache, embarrassment, or disappointment; emotions so raw it is hard to express. Let me be clear, there is nothing wrong with general prayers, but when we have a relationship with God through our faith in Jesus Christ, we have an intimate connection.

When we pray specifically, we trust God with all of the pain, doubt, worry, and fear we are carrying. When we pray specifically, we are trusting our deepest secrets to the One who loves us unconditionally. When we pray specifically, it helps our spirit avoid drowning in the grief that swirls around us. When we pray specifically, we place our expectations on the belief that God knows what is best for us. A specific prayer is a serious prayer.

"Do not be anxious about anything, but in everything by prayer and supplication with thanksgiving let your requests be made known to God"(Philippians 4:6).

As we pray specifically, we should quote scripture and pray it back to God. It's one of the keys to asking God for help! The following are three kinds of scriptures you should quote back to God:

1. Quote scriptures that express grief or sorrow.
2. Quote scriptures that tell the truth about God.
3. Quote scriptures that talk about the promises of God.

Make a point to study the Word of God every single day so, like Jonah, you can pray the Lord's life-giving words back to Him. And as you do, the Lord, your God, will bring hope and peace back into your life.

Jonah 2:2

"I called out to the LORD, out of my distress, and he answered me; out of the belly of Sheol I cried, and you heard my voice."

Note that the second half of the verse is parallel, in meaning, to the first half of the verse; it repeats the ideas conveyed. Scholars call this Synonymous Parallelism. This literary device is frequently used in Hebrew poetry. It is found throughout the poetic sections and in the wisdom literature in the Bible, such as Moses' Song of Farewell in Deuteronomy 32:1-43 and the Song of the Sea in Exodus 15:1-18.

The prophet Jonah compared the fish's belly to a burial chamber from which he could not escape. He called to God from Sheol, yet he was not in Sheol.

Sheol is found in the Bible sixty-five times. It is translated as "the pit" three times, "the grave" thirty-one times, and "hell" thirty-one times. In this verse, Sheol is translated as the grave.

Commentator Ibn Ezra explains that "Sheol is a deep dark place which is opposite of the heavens which are on high." In other words, the term Sheol is used to describe the depths of the earth, a gravely place, a place far from the presence of God.

In Jonah's mind, he is as distant from God as an individual can be.

Many ancient religions share an image of a lower world to which the dead go. In Greek mythology, the underworld lies across the river Styx, often called Hades, after the god who ruled there. However, Hades is not the same as Sheol. Remember, Sheol is understood as a biblical metaphor for the destination of the dead, not a physical location.

Here in this verse, Jonah declares that he was near death, but now that he has been rescued from the sea, he thanks the Lord. The verse does not speak of general distress. Jonah calls out to God as a result of his very specific pain.

Pray Passionately

Jonah can teach us a lot about praying passionately, but what does it mean to pray passionately? First, let's look at what a passionate prayer is not.

Passionate prayer is not a prayer where you can barely keep awake while you're praying. Passionate prayer is not a prayer where you're thinking about something else while the words of prayer come from your mouth. Passionate prayer is an earnestly and emotionally involved prayer.

As Jonah dropped down into the ocean and got swallowed by a big fish, he said, "out of the belly of Sheol, I cried." Jonah does this because he knows God answers desperate and emotional prayers. In the Bible, that's called lamenting. It means to express sorrow, remorse, or disappointment over something strongly. In fact, many of the psalms are laments, prayers of grievance to God.

God wants you to pray with your heart, soul, and mind. He always knows when His children say something they don't mean. The Lord always knows when His children are speaking with a genuine heart. God cares about your discomfort, pain, and frustration. He wants to hear what's on your heart.

Our heavenly Father would rather listen to your grievances than to a well-mannered prayer you don't really mean. And if you find yourself in a challenging situation right now, skip the routine and predictable prayer and share your heart with the Lord. He wants to hear you pray passionately. Passionate prayers move God, and when God is moved, He moves mountains.

Jonah 2:3-5

"For you cast me into the deep, into the heart of the seas, and the flood surrounded me; all your waves and your billows passed over me. Then I said, I am driven away from your sight; yet I shall again look upon your holy temple. The waters closed in over me to take my life; the deep surrounded me; weeds were wrapped about my head at the roots of the mountains."

The text addressed to the Lord says, "For you cast me into the deep." We know from previous verses that the sailors cast Jonah into the sea. However, Jonah saw God's disciplinary hand behind the sailors who had only been the Lord's tools in casting the prophet into the sea.

Jonah acknowledged that the sea belonged to God, and the waves overwhelmed him many times before the fish swallowed him. This condition made Jonah believe that God turned His back on him. Nevertheless, he was determined to seek God in prayer. "Look upon your holy temple" means that Jonah thought he would gaze upon God's dwelling place of holiness and that the gift of prophecy would return to him.

As is often the case, the biblical text does not provide many details. The text does not tell us how long Jonah was in the water before the fish swallowed him. Yet, we know from the text that Jonah sensed his hopelessness and continued his downward plunge into the deep. He seemed to be in death's grip rather than God's hands, and seaweeds bound his head as the water encased his body.

Jonah 2:6-7

"I went down to the land whose bars closed upon me forever; yet you brought up my life from the pit, O LORD my God. When my life was fainting away, I remembered the LORD, and my prayer came to you, into your holy temple."

The first phrase of verse 6 describes the depths of Jonah's descent. The prophet descended in the sea to the bottoms of the mountains. He was as low as one can go. There he felt imprisoned like a prisoner, powerless and unable to escape.

As Jonah felt that his life was fading away and his death was approaching, he turned his thoughts toward God. Even though he felt far from God, he remembered the Lord's authority and prayed. Amazingly, his passionate prayer reached God in His heavenly dwelling place.

Remember What God Has Done

As I've recently been studying the book of Psalm, I've discovered that Psalms 77 will genuinely take you to the heart of prayer, admiration, thankfulness, and worship. For example, Psalms 77:11 says, ***"I will remember the deeds of the Lord; yes, I will remember your wonders of old."*** The author of this psalm shows us that when we are in a low place, and it seems that finding God is difficult, remembering what He has done for us in the past helps us trust that God will meet us in our present circumstance also. That is precisely what Jonah did when he felt his life was slipping away. He remembered the Lord's faithfulness.

When we are facing challenging times and feeling overwhelmed, worry and fear are a natural human response. Nevertheless, instead of worrying, the Lord wants us to remember who He is and remember what He has done. In fact, remembering what God has done for us in the past is an opportunity to offer Him praise in the present. Remembering the works of God in our past, keeps our minds and hearts focused on Him.

God is faithful in the ups and downs. And as you remember to give thanks during difficult times and hardships, you're reminded that God never changes, and He has never left you, no matter the circumstance. Sometimes, remembering what God has done in your life is the very thing you need to pick yourself up when you are feeling down.

Psalms 16:8 says, ***"I have set the Lord always before me; because he is at my right hand, I shall not be shaken."*** Therefore, set the ways of the Lord before you, and focus on

His love, strength, character, and authority. Be encouraged to write down your walk with the Lord so that you can remember His goodness. Remember God's incredible power and His unconditional love for you! God can handle anything, including whatever you are dealing with right now. Rest assured that what the Lord did in the past, He can surely do again.

Jonah 2:8-9

"Those who pay regard to vain idols forsake their hope of steadfast love. But I with the voice of thanksgiving will sacrifice to you; what I have vowed I will pay. Salvation belongs to the LORD!"

During his prayer, Jonah mentioned the word "idols." He was referring to the sailors as "those who pay regard to vain idols." The men of the ship were calling out and inspiring one another in their acts of idolatry. The sailors did not only uphold their idolatrous worship; they enthusiastically guarded it. They clung to it.

Jonah's desperate condition brought him to his senses. He simply thanked God for saving his life and returned to his worship of God with a sacrifice. He also promised to pay his vow to God.

Even though the text does not tell us what the vow is, I believe this vow refers to his commitment to serve the Lord faithfully. Furthermore, I believe he vows to go to Nineveh with a voice of gratitude and proclaim what he had been commanded.

The last declaration in this prayer is one of the most fantastic summary statements about salvation in the Bible. The testimony that salvation comes from the Lord is an expression of Jonah's thanksgiving. This statement in the prayer also acknowledges that God has the right to save whom He will.

The Lure of Idols

We tend to think of idolatry as a sin of the past or an old religious thing. However, idolatry is astonishingly modern and very prevalent in our culture. Part of the reason we do not think about idol worship today is that our understanding of idolatry is incorrect. We think idolatry is limited to bowing down to a golden statue or praying to a wooden trinket. Since we don't do those things, we assume we are not practicing idolatry.

An idol is anything more significant to you than God. It is anything that absorbs your heart and imagination more than the Lord. Lastly, an idol is anything that you pursue to give you what only God can provide.

We live in a society filled with potential idols, things we make so vital that we push God and His purposes for us to the back burner. For example, we often make idols out of wealth, success, or possessions. We can even make great and beautiful things into idols, such as our marriages, our families, or even our ministries in the church. Many of us also idolize our country and ourselves.

Furthermore, trusting in someone or something other than God can have devastating effects on our lives. If we think our relationships, possessions, or what we do will make us completely fulfilled, we set ourselves up for profound disappointment and failure. None of those things can give us meaning in life or provide total security. Sadly, idols don't just stop after they have disappointed us; eventually, they enslave us, too.

The Bible says, ***"Those who make them become like them; so do all who trust in them" (Psalm 115:8).***

Whatever you value the most in life, you are going to become like. If you value money more than God, money becomes your idol, and you will ultimately become avaricious. If you value pleasure, you will eventually become hedonistic. But if you value Jesus Christ, above all, and believe that He rose from the dead, you will become a Christian.

Make it your goal today to have a deep and intimate relationship with God through your faith in Jesus Christ. Allow Him into every area of your life. When you choose to serve God with your whole heart and make Him first in your life, your soul will flourish, and your joy and peace will increase.

Remember to lean on the Lord more than anything else, and He will put everything else in perspective. If you take it one day at a time, you and the Lord together can do and achieve anything!

Jonah 2:10

"And the LORD spoke to the fish, and it vomited Jonah out upon the dry land."

Again, Jonah glorified God by ascribing control of the large fish to Him. The text says, "The Lord spoke to the fish," but unlike Jonah, the fish obeyed God and vomited the disobedient prophet onto dry land. Jonah had spoken to the Lord in confession, and now God responded by speaking to the fish in deliverance. Having gained a preview of Sheol, Jonah was now ready to go to the Ninevites, whose destiny was Sheol.

God's dramatic intervention in saving Jonah gives hope– not only for those who seek the Lord but also for those, who like Jonah, have determined to shut him out.

Scholars and theologians do not know precisely where Jonah was dumped on dry land. However, first-century Romano-Jewish historian, Flavius Josephus, stated that it was upon the Euxine Seashore, which we know as the Black Sea. If that was true, the great fish passed through the Dardanelles before vomiting him, thus following the strong current mentioned in Jonah's prayer.

The following table shows how this chapter parallels with chapter 1 in its contents.

Chapter 1: The Sailors	Chapter 2: The Prophet
1:4 Crisis on the sea	**2:3-6** Crisis in the sea
1:14 Prayer to God	**2:2-9** Prayer to God
1:15 Deliverance from the storm on the sea	**2:10** Deliverance from the fish in the sea
1:16 Sacrifice and vows offered to God	**2:9** Sacrifice and vows offered to God

Please Forgive Me, Lord

As Christians, it is safe to say the Lord plays a vital role in our lives. We worship God with our praise, our prayers, and by studying His words. There is no doubt we do our very best to live fruitful and godly lives as devoted followers of Jesus Christ. Nevertheless, perfection will always escape us, no matter how much we worship God and follow His instructions.

As long as you are on this earth, you will make mistakes; you will always struggle against temptation. However, there is some good news: God is loving, merciful, and ready to forgive you for your wrongdoings. But let me make this clear: God forgives you not because you are good but because He is good. He is a good God, and He has a good plan for you, even when you mess up big time.

Even though God is eager to forgive the sins of His children, merely asking is not enough. There are several essential steps that you must take. Here in chapter two, Jonah gives us a blueprint to God's forgiveness:

- **Step 1. Acknowledge Your Sins**
- **Step 2. Confess to God**
- **Step 3. Ask God for Forgiveness**
- **Step 4. Change Your Behavior**
- **Step 5. Obey God's Will for Your Life**

As long as you are honest in your commitment to move beyond your mistakes, God will forgive you for your transgressions and help you to lead a better life in His image. Always remember, the price has been paid, and you do not have to go through life feeling guilty and condemned. You are receiving forgiveness, by faith, through the love, grace, and mercy of Jesus Christ.

Chapter 3

Jonah Preaches

Second Commission of Jonah

Jonah 3:1

"Then the word of the LORD came to Jonah the second time, saying,"

Jonah did not clarify precisely when this second commission came to him. It may have been immediately after Jonah reached dry land, or it may have been sometime later. Nonetheless, we clearly see in the text that God gave Jonah another opportunity. Therefore, let us dig a little bit deeper into Jonah's second chance.

God saved Jonah from drowning, and Jonah repented for his sin. But that does not mean that God had to send Jonah to Nineveh. God does not always give His servants a second chance to obey Him when they refuse to do so initially. Often, He simply uses other individuals or other things to accomplish His purposes.

God could have quickly sent Jonah home and called another individual to be a prophet to the Ninevites. The Lord could have recruited a brand-new prophet for this mission. Or, God could have sent a more reliable veteran prophet who had already demonstrated loyalty, someone like Elijah. However,

God gave Jonah a second chance, a second chance for Jonah to emerge from the fish with a renewed mind.

God put Jonah in precisely the same position described in the very first verse of the book of Jonah. The first time God called Jonah, Jonah fled. Now, the second time, God called Jonah and expects that Jonah will act differently. This second chance is genuine and complete forgiveness.

Thank God for Second Chances

Sometimes it is hard for people to believe they can be forgiven. Nevertheless, the Lord shows us several examples in the Bible of individuals being forgiven and receiving another opportunity to right their wrongs. One of those examples is here in the book of Jonah.

God gives Jonah a second chance, and if He did it for Jonah, I believe He will provide you with one also. Why? Because God is the God of the second chance, the hundredth chance, and the thousandth chance!

The Lord, our God, is a loving Father. No matter how rebellious we have been, no matter what has happened in the past or how low we have fallen, He always stands ready to forgive us. It is essential to understand that God's second chances reflect His grace, mercy, and love for us.

But what do you do when God does give you another opportunity?

When you receive another opportunity, please don't waste it. Your second chance is an excellent time to focus on God's unique calling for your life. And with the Lord's help, you can look at yourself, repent, make amends, and begin again. When God gives you a second chance, I want you to adopt a lifestyle of thankfulness.

I want you to live gratefully! Wake up every day with profound gratitude for the opportunity the Lord has given you. The Bible says in Psalm 92:1-2, ***"It is good to give thanks to the Lord, to sing praises to your name, O Most High, to declare your steadfast love in the morning, and your faithfulness by night."*** When you live with an attitude of praise and gratefulness, you shield yourself from the enemy's attacks. Seeds of discouragement cannot take root in a thankful heart.

Therefore, renew your mind and be empowered with God's strength to overcome in every area of your life! A second chance is a significant step toward your spiritual growth. A second chance shows you it is not too late to become everything you were created to be.

If you start right where you are, glorifying God, being your very best, and serving others, the right doors will open, the right people will show up because your second chance is covered by love.

Jonah 3:2-3

"Arise, go to Nineveh, that great city, and call out against it the message that I tell you." So Jonah arose and went to Nineveh, according to the word of the LORD. Now Nineveh was an exceedingly great city, three days' journey in breadth."

Let me ask you the same question from chapter 1, have you ever wondered why God would send Jonah to deliver a message to the people of a non-Israelite city? A nation of people who weren't in covenant with our heavenly Father?

The assignment of Jonah was not for the advantage of the people of Nineveh. Instead, God's concern for Nineveh is really out of concern for Israel. After Jonah's prophecy, Assyria will be prepared to be an instrument of God's rage to discipline Israel, who deserved punishment for their disobedience. Our heavenly Father wanted the Assyrians to repent so that they would be ready to fulfill His decree on Israel.

God wanted to demonstrate that Nineveh possesses greater merit than Israel because they listened to His chosen prophet's words and repented. At the same time, Israel hardens their hearts towards God's chosen prophets and ignores God's warnings.

Note: This was the sign of Jonah, Jesus was referring to in Matthew 12:39. The sign of Jonah was that the Word of God would be spoken to Gentiles, and Gentiles would hear it and repent. This sign was revealed and confirmed in Acts 10:1-48 when Peter witnessed God pouring out His spirit on Cornelius and his household after Peter proclaimed the gospel.

The biblical text does not record Jonah saying a word in response to God's renewed call to go to Nineveh. Furthermore, we do not get a lot of specific details about his journey. Did Jonah walk to Nineveh by himself? How long did it take Jonah to get from the seashore to Nineveh? However, we do know that Jonah obeyed God this time and traveled east to Nineveh.

Often stories in the Bible leave us wanting to know more. The only detail the text does provide is the mention of "a three-day journey" at the conclusion of the verse. The meaning behind the "three-day journey" remains somewhat unclear.

Some Jewish and Christian commentators take it to mean that Jonah walked three days from where the fish left him on dry land to reach Nineveh. However, historians familiar with the Middle East's geography understand that no one could walk the hundreds of miles from the Mediterranean coast to Nineveh in three days. Another explanation is that the literal meaning of the phrase "three-day journey" describes the protocol involved in visiting a significant city such as Nineveh. In the ancient Near East, it was customary for a messenger from another nation to take three days for an official visit.

I believe the "three-day journey" describes the time it took to visit the city and its outlying suburbs. This phrase points to Nineveh's geographical size as being large and requiring quite a few days for Jonah's message to reach everyone.

Note: Nineveh had a perimeter of approximately eight miles. It would take a considerable amount of time for Jonah to walk around and speak at different points on this trip.

Jonah 3:4

"Jonah began to go into the city, going a day's journey. And he called out, "Yet forty days, and Nineveh shall be overthrown!"

When Jonah proceeded into the city, he began announcing his message from the Lord during the first day. The essence of his proclamation was that Nineveh would be overthrown in only 40 days. However, let's look closely at the wording of Jonah's proclamation.

The more literal translation for the word "overthrown" is the Hebrew word *"nehpachet,"* which means to overturned. In other words, Jonah is not proclaiming that if the Ninevites do not repent, they will be overthrown in forty days. He is declaring that in forty days, Nineveh will be overturned, one way or another.

Jonah's proclamation can be understood in two ways:

1. There will be overturning through their deeds, from evil to good, from misdeeds to righteousness.
2. There will be overturning like that of Sodom and Gomorrah.

If Nineveh repents and overturns their deeds by turning to the God of Israel, then the overturning of destruction will be avoided.

Let me say it this way: Nineveh is indeed overturned, not by divine destruction but by the repentance of the people of Nineveh.

Respect the Warning Signs

What can we learn from the Ninevites?

Can we turn our lives around when we get warnings?

It is essential to pay attention to signs and warnings. Just about wherever we go, we will come in contact with some type of warning, whether in the form of declarations, symbols, lights, or labels. We are frequently ruled and measured by these warnings, like the ones we receive from the police, governments, doctors, employers, and spouses. Not heeding these warnings can result in some pretty significant consequences.

Too often, we choose to ignore the warnings until it is too late. We wait until our health can no longer be recovered. We delay until our relationships can no longer be restored. However, if we pay attention to these warnings signs and respect the guidelines, rules, and laws in place, we can have better, healthier, and safer lives.

The same goes for warnings from the Lord. God loves you enough to give you a warning sign. Are you paying attention?

God wants you to have a wonderful and fruitful life. Therefore, respect the warning signs. God is trying to protect you from heartache and sorrow.

Jonah 3:5

"And the people of Nineveh believed God."

Have you ever asked yourself why the Ninevites believed?

I have always wondered why the Ninevites were so quick to believe Jonah's warning. Would you consider someone's warning of destruction? A person who you do not know, who comes from another country speaking a different language? What if that person had a different faith and worshiped a different god? Would you believe that person, especially when you consider them an enemy?

Commentator Ibn Ezra explains that what is reported in this verse is not an abstract theological statement that the Ninevites believed in the existence of the God of Israel. Instead, they believed that "the word of God," as spoken by Jonah, was real and accurate. They believed that Nineveh was about to be destroyed because they recognized Jonah as an authentic representative of the God of Israel.

David Kimchi explains why the Ninevites respond so dramatically to Jonah's words:

> For the men of the ship were in the city, and they gave testimony concerning him. They told the story

> of the storm and admitted that they had thrown him into the sea. Therefore, the Ninevites believed in his prophecy and repented.

Rabbi Malbim offers an alternative view:

> And, notably, they believed instantly, and they did not ask for a sign or a miracle. They immediately began to pray through the means that they put on sackcloth to fast and be humble. And the nation was not roused to repentance because it did not occur to them that they were sinners. After all, Jonah had not informed them of this.

I find it interesting David Kimchi thinks the Ninevites believed Jonah's words because of evidence. At the same time, Rabbi Malbim thinks the Ninevites accepted Jonah's words without question because, for the first time, they saw the evil of their ways. So, I guess another question to ask is, in whom did the Ninevites believe? Jewish statesman Isaac Abarbanel distinguishes between belief in God and belief in Jonah:

> Jonah explains this proclamation concerning their sins in general and in detail about the violence of their deeds. And they turned to the Lord, and God had mercy. They accepted the words of Jonah to

> become good and proper. Thus, it says, "And the people of Nineveh believed God." It does not say that they believed Jonah. Instead, it says that they believed God, that it was in His hands to bring the destruction of Nineveh, and that He loves the righteous, and He hates violence. The words of Jonah awake them to perform their repentance.

I agree with Abarbanel because rarely does the Old Testament speak of people having faith in God. Instead, it focuses on the questions of how people act rather than what they believe.

Note: Assyrians had practiced a religion called Ashurism. Ashurism was the first religion of the Assyrians. In its Latin form, the very word Assyrian derives from the name of Ashur, the Assyrian god. Assyrians continued to practice Ashurism until 256 A.D. However, most Assyrians had accepted Christianity by that time. In 33 A.D., the Assyrian Church was founded by apostles Thomas, Bartholomew, and Thaddeus.

Let's return to the opening question: Why did the Ninevites believe Jonah's brief proclamation? I want to approach this question from a different perspective, and I think the timing of Jonah's message is the key.

The Ninevites were consumed by two plagues that had ravaged Nineveh in 765 and 759 B.C., a severe flood and a famine. A total eclipse of the sun also occurred in 763 B.C. The total eclipse would have impacted their belief because a significant part of their faith was that Ashur, their god, was a solar deity. Therefore, I believe these occurrences prepared the Ninevites for Jonah's message. The Ninevites viewed these occurrences as indications of divine displeasure, a common reaction in the ancient Near East.

The Ninevites must have already believed on a subconscious level that their actions were unacceptable by their gods. Consequently, when Jonah began proclaiming that Nineveh would be overthrown in 40 days, they believed in the God of Israel. They thought it was in His authority to bring destruction to their land and people. They saw Jonah's message as an intervention for their misbehavior.

Faith Is More Than Just Believing

When you say you believe in Jesus, what do you mean? Why do you have faith in Jesus? Do you believe in Jesus because your parents have faith? Do you believe because someone told you what you should believe?

Did you know Satan believes in Jesus? So, do demons. Nevertheless, you will not discover any of them in Heaven. Why? Because saying you believe in Jesus does not mean you have faith in Him. It also doesn't mean you completely trust Him to lead your life as the divine authority of God.

James 2:18-26 teaches us that faith is more than just intellectual knowledge. Faith is also something you do. It is active, not passive. Real faith includes making a vow to trust in Christ and allow Him to be king over your life.

In other words, the Apostle James is saying that our belief and commitment to Jesus should change us, and it is reflected in the things we do. Real faith shows up in our lifestyles. Our good deeds are indications of our genuine and unquestioning devotion to the Lord.

Now, this does not mean we can earn our salvation. The Bible says in Ephesians 2:8-9, ***"For by grace you have been saved through faith. And this is not your own doing; it is the gift of God, not a result of works, so that no one may boast."*** We are saved by faith in Jesus, the risen Messiah, nothing more and nothing less.

So, what can you do today to show others your faith in Jesus? You can serve them, support them, encourage them, and even show them how your faith is changing you. There is no better time than right now to take a stand for Jesus Christ and demonstrate your faith.

You are God's masterpiece. You are here to be the light. So, why would you hide? The Lord is not a secret to be kept. It is time for you to shine! Be generous with your life and with sharing the good news of Christ. By opening up to others, you will prompt people to open up to God, our generous Father in Heaven.

Jonah 3:5-6

"And the people of Nineveh believed God. They called for a fast and put on sackcloth, from the greatest of them to the least of them. The word reached the king of Nineveh, and he arose from his throne, removed his robe, covered himself with sackcloth, and sat in ashes."

Jonah's proclamation moved the Ninevites to humble themselves and seek divine mercy and grace. Despite the Ninevites' wickedness, they were open to God's message, and they began to repent. The people of Nineveh did not wait for the king to declare a fast. In fact, they started repenting for their evil before the king of Nineveh received notice of what was happening in the city. They took their own initiative, and the king took his cue from the people's response.

Fasting and wearing sackcloth demonstrated self-affliction, which reflected an attitude of humility in the ancient Near East. Sackcloth was the garment that the underprivileged and the slaves customarily wore. Thus, wearing it portrayed that the entire population regarded themselves as servants. Nonetheless, the king took it one step further.

The king of Nineveh would probably have been the king of Assyria since Nineveh was a leading city of the Assyrian empire. Scholars believe Ashur-dan III was most likely the king during this time. Ashur-dan III was king of Assyria from 773 B.C. to 755 B.C.

Ashur-dan's reign was a difficult time for the Assyrian monarchy. According to the Assyrian eponym canon, in 765 B.C., Assyria was hit by a plague. In 763 B.C., an insurgency broke out, which lasted until 759 B.C., when another plague devastated the land. His reign and the reigns of preceding Assyrian kings have been astronomically dated based on the only verifiable reference to a solar eclipse in Assyrian chronicles, the so-called eclipse of Bur Sagale.

The following table shows the Assyrian kings during Jonah's prophetic ministry:

Assyrian Kings	
Adad-nirari III	**810 - 783 B.C.**
Shalmaneser IV	**783 - 773 B.C.**
Ashur-dan III	**773 - 755 B.C.**
Ashur-nirari V	**755 - 745 B.C.**

The ancient Assyrians did not believe that their king was divine himself but saw their ruler as the vicar of their principal deity. Specifically, Assyrians believed the king was appointed directly through divine right by the chief deity, Ashur. They saw their king as Ashur's top representative on Earth. Furthermore, the Assyrians thought the king was the link between the gods and the earthly realm. As such, it was the king's paramount responsibility to learn the will of the gods, build temples, and wage war.

In their worldview, Assyria represented a place of order while lands not governed by the Assyrian king (and, by extension, the god Ashur) were seen as places of chaos and disorder. It was seen as the king's duty to expand the borders of Assyria and bring order and civilization to lands perceived as uncivilized.

In verse 6, King Ashur-dan III could have stubbornly refused to follow the lead of his people. But instead, he acts with humility and wisdom by repenting and humbling himself as a servant. The text tells us that he literally rose from his throne and removed his robe, which means he "removed his glory and renders his honor." The king follows the example of the people and puts on sackcloth, and then adopts an ancient Hebrew custom by sitting in ashes, a sign of repentance.

Results of Obedience

Jonah 3:7-8

"And he issued a proclamation and published through Nineveh, "By the decree of the king and his nobles: Let neither man nor beast, herd nor flock, taste anything. Let them not feed or drink water, but let man and beast be covered with sackcloth, and let them call out mightily to God. Let everyone turn from his evil way and from the violence that is in his hands."

Verses 7-8 further describes how seriously the king and his nobles regarded their circumstances and to what extent they went to inspire citywide repentance. However, verse 7 begins with a problematic phrase. As we have seen in earlier chapters, the English translation masks the difficulties of the original Hebrew text.

In the original Hebrew, the verse begins by using the word *"Vayazeik,"* which means cried out. Therefore, the king did not passively issue a proclamation. But with his kingly authority, King Ashur-dan III swiftly demanded that the repentance be publicly proclaimed by making it an official government policy.

Our verse also uses the word "decree," but in the original Hebrew, the term is *"ta'am,"* which means "from his advice, his knowledge, his wisdom, and his discernment." Therefore, the text is actually saying, "By the advice, knowledge, wisdom, and discernment of the king and his nobles: Let neither man nor beast, herd nor flock, taste anything."

The interesting part of this passage comes in the wide-ranging application of the order to fast. Not only did all the people of Nineveh fast, but the animals fasted as well. But why do the animals have to fast? The king and his nobles did not regard animals as needing to humble themselves through fasting but viewed animals as expressing their owners' spirit. Consequently, by everyone and everything fasting, the king hopes the change will take place. But to understand how the Ninevites change, we need to look a bit more closely at the extent of their evil and the nature of their repentance.

In verse 8, we learn that not only did the animals fast, but they also wore sackcloth. Furthermore, this verse's first sentence shows us that they called out mightily to the God of Israel. But who called out mightily to God? From the sentence structure, one might conclude the people and the animals called out to Israel's God.

In the last sentence in verse 8, we see the word violence, which was translated from the Hebrew word *"chamas."* Chamas refers to the overbearing attitude and conduct of someone who has attained power over others and misuses it. Chamas is the word that the book of Genesis uses to describe Noah's generation and Sodom's population. Using the term *"chamas"* here, the author puts the sins of the Ninevites in the same category as those of the generation of Noah and the people of Sodom.

French Rabbi Rashi suggests the Ninevites were so violent that they even used violence to appeal to God. He provides an imaginative interpretation of the word "mightily." Most readers take it to describe the intensity or passion of the appeal by Ninevites, but Rashi understands mightily to mean "with might and force." Rashi suggests the Ninevites used an act of mighty violence, embodied by experiments of death, to state their case to God.

However, unlike Rashi, Rabbi Kimchi understands mightily to mean "with all their hearts." Calling out to the God of Israel with all their hearts would have been a rare and strange practice for them because Ashur was their supreme deity, and no other god was more significant in their belief.

Love God with Your All

When Jesus was asked about the most important commandment, He made it very simple for us when He said, ***"You must love the Lord your God with all your heart, all your soul, all your mind, and all your strength" (Mark 12:30).***

Christ draws no division between these four elements. And neither should we. We should work hard to excel in all of them. But what does loving God with all your heart, soul, mind, and strength mean?

As Christians, we speak about how we love God, but do we? Do we love the Lord with our all? In other words, do we love God above any other individual, creature, or object in our lives? I want you to examine the depths of your heart and soul.

Think about what your response will be to the above questions. Once again, can you say that you love God with your "whole heart" and with all that is within you? Remember, God knows you better than you know yourself, so answer honestly.

Loving God with all your heart, soul, mind, and strength means to love God with your spirit, body, emotions, will, and intellect. Loving God with all your heart, soul, mind, and strength means to love Him at all times, even when it seems He is a million miles away and even when you are going through difficult times. Loving the Lord with all your heart, soul, mind, and strength means to love Him even when your prayers aren't answered as you hoped they would be. Loving God with all your heart, soul, mind, and strength means to love the Lord when He says yes, no, or wait.

When you fully love God, you won't put another god or idol before Him. You won't take His name in vain. You will only seek to love Him and do what He wants you to do. When you put God front and center in your life, you will truly begin loving yourself and others. When you love God first, everything else in your life will fall in line accordingly. A blessed life all starts with loving God with your all.

Jonah 3:9-10

"Who knows? God may turn and relent and turn from his fierce anger, so that we may not perish." When God saw what they did, how they turned from their evil way, God relented of the disaster that he had said he would do to them, and he did not do it."

The original Hebrew text is unclear to whom our verse's opening phrase, "Who knows," refers to. It could be read as a rhetorical question, as in "Who knows?" Several Jewish and Christian commentators take a different approach. They read it as a declarative phrase meaning "He who knows."

Rashi understands the sentence's subject to be, not God, but rather those Ninevites who are sinners. Rabbi Kimchi offers two ways to read the phrase:

> Who knows, perhaps God will have mercy on us in response to our repentance from our evil deeds. Or, it could also be explained, the ones who know the paths of repentance will repent, and the God of Blessing will have mercy.

Abarbanel also presents two ways of understanding this phrase:

> This means to say, "who knows which specific act of exploitation and robbery was done by the hand

> of which specific Ninevite that he will repent of it." It could also mean who knows which of the paths of repentance one should follow to repent before the Lord so that He will be merciful to them".

Based on the passage's context, Kimchi's first thought makes the most sense to me. Wrapped up in two words, "Who knows," King Ashur-dan III was saying, "Who knows but that God may turn and relent? He may turn back from His wrath, so we do not perish." The king does not promise the Ninevites that these acts of repentance will save them. He does not begin this sentence, "I know." Instead, he humbly tells his people that this might work.

The Ninevites and the king joined together to envision the possibility of being saved. They did not know with certainty that God would forgive them if they repented. Jonah had not structured his proclamation as a conditional statement. He did not say, "If you do not repent in the next forty days, Nineveh will be destroyed." The king and the people of Nineveh imagined the only path leading to their survival was to repent.

In verse 10, God saw their repentance. But what precisely did God see?

He saw the genuineness of the Ninevites' repentance in their hearts and a shift in their actions. These fruits of repentance moved the Lord to withhold the judgment He would have sent on them had they persisted in their wicked ways.

One might have expected that the Ninevites' complete repentance described in this chapter would also include them renouncing the worship of idols and accepting the one true God. But the chapter contains no such mention. Like the sailors' actions in chapter 1, this repentance does not necessarily convert the people of Nineveh to the one true God. It merely postpones the inevitable.

Note: In 612 B.C., Nineveh was sacked and burned by an alliance of Babylonians, Persians, Medes, and Scythians. And by 609 B.C., the Assyrian Empire was completely overthrown and destroyed.

What It Means to Repent

When you hear the word "repent," what is the first thing you think about? How does the word make you feel? For many people, the word "repent" is negative and undesirable. When those individuals hear that word, they think about the person holding a sign on the corner telling everyone to "repent or burn in Hell" because the end is near. But the world's idea of what it means to repent is incorrect. "Repent" is essentially one of the most encouraging and transforming words in the world.

Furthermore, many of us are taught that the word "repent" means that you change your mind. However, that meaning is incorrect. The term "repent" comes from the Hebrew word *"teshuvah,"* which means "return." Repentance means you used to think or act one way, and now you return to your true essence.

For example, if you are having fearful thoughts, return to your true essence of perfect love because it casts out all fear. If you are worried and stressed, return to your true essence of perfect peace by praying with gratefulness in your heart, letting your requests be made known to God. If you are selfish, return to your true essence of perfect humility by counting others more significant than yourself, looking not only to your own interests but also to the interests of others. If you've sinned, ask God for forgiveness and return to your true essence of worship and worship God in spirit and truth. For the Christian, return to your true essence of love, loving the Lord your God and loving your neighbor as yourself.

The path to a fresh start and a clear conscience begins with daily repentance. In fact, the formula for true repentance is found in a very familiar passage:

If my people, which are called by my name, shall humble themselves, and pray, and seek my face, and turn from their wicked ways; then will I hear from heaven, and will forgive their sin, and will heal their land (2 Chronicles 7:14).

Furthermore, Acts 3:19 says, ***"Repent therefore, and turn again, that your sins may be blotted out…".***

Repentance returns you to God, creates the possibility of new thinking, and leads to a unique perspective that empowers a different approach. When you repent and return to your true essence, it's not about not getting to do the things you want to do anymore. It's about doing only the things that matter because your mind and heart are set on what's most important, God's will.

Chapter 4

Jonah Pouts

Prejudice of Jonah

Jonah 4:1

"But it displeased Jonah exceedingly, and he was angry."

One of the questions driving the story of Jonah from the beginning has been: What will happen to the city of Nineveh, whose wickedness is so great that it grabs the attention of the God of Israel? That issue has now been resolved. The people of Nineveh heard the prophetic word, the repentance and good deeds of the Ninevites pleased God, and they rearranged their lives.

However, another question remains. What will happen to a prophet who disobeys the Lord? Jonah has discovered that it is impossible to run away from God. His preaching in Nineveh seemed amazingly fruitful. One would think he would be ecstatic, but Jonah is displeased.

But why did it displease Jonah? Why did Jonah become angry when God spared Nineveh? Who was he to complain after his disobedience?

A straightforward reading of this verse would understand Jonah to be expressing a self-centered and wounded pride. He had declared the coming destruction of Nineveh, but God forgave the Ninevites. This approach is consistent with the selfish personal traits expressed by Jonah in chapter 1. But let's dig deeper into why Jonah was displeased and angry that God spared Nineveh.

There are two reasons why Jonah was displeased and angry:

1. Jonah was displeased because he thought that God would not forgive Nineveh unless they repented their evil ways in faith (idol worship) and deeds (violence). But Jonah saw that Nineveh remained firm in their idol worship and did not repent from their idol worship but, instead, only repented for their actions against each other. And despite this, the Lord was merciful.
2. Jonah undeniably became angry because he wanted God to judge the Ninevites and remove the military threat to the nation of Israel. If Jonah were aware of Hosea and Amos' prophecies, he would have known that Assyria would attack and overthrow Israel (Hosea 11:5; Amos 5:27).

"They shall not return to the land of Egypt, but Assyria shall be their king, because they have refused to return to me" (Hosea 11:5).

"You shall take up Sikkuth your king, and Kiyyun your star-god—your images that you made for yourselves, and I will send you into exile beyond Damascus," says the Lord, whose name is the God of hosts" Amos 5: 26-27).

It is safe to assume that Jonah's disappointment stemmed from his knowledge of the Ninevites' role in the future destruction of the Northern Kingdom of Israel.

Note: In 722 B.C., the Assyrians conquered Israel. The Assyrian army captured the Israelite capital at Samaria and carried the citizens of the northern Kingdom of Israel away into captivity. Israel's destruction left the southern kingdom, Judah, to fend for itself among warring Near-Eastern kingdoms. (See 1 Chronicles 5:26, 2 Kings 17:5-6)

Why You Should Always Forgive

When those you love upset and hurt you, are you willing to forgive them in the way that God forgave Jonah? This question is an essential question for you to answer because if you are unwilling to forgive someone and don't want God to forgive them either, that reveals a level of resentment and bitterness, and a degree of hatred in your heart. Furthermore, if you are unwilling to forgive, why should the Lord forgive you for all the wrong things you have done? Remember what Jesus said, ***"but if you do not forgive others their trespasses, neither will your Father forgive your trespasses" (Matthew 6:15).***

Forgiveness involves your past, present, and future, which means God has forgiven you numerous times in the past, He will forgive you for the slipups you make today, and He will forgive you for the mistakes you commit tomorrow. But you have to do your part and forgive other people's past, present, and future. Let me be clear; forgiveness doesn't mean what an individual did was right. Forgiveness separates the offense from the offender and humbly releases the debt they owe you so God can remove the debt you owe Him. Your lack of forgiveness is not hurting them; it is only hurting you.

Have you ever thought about how much energy it takes to be bitter or hold resentment? You only have a certain amount of energy each day. If you use it for the wrong purpose or magnify the negativity in your life and dwell on whoever hurt you, you will not have the energy to make the best decisions or be as creative as you need to be. You will not be able to live your best life! Therefore, decide to make what Jesus did FOR you more significant than what they did TO you. Forgive them, let it go, and refocus on God's plan for your life.

Lastly, start seeing people as God sees people. Shift your perspective and change the lenses in your spiritual glasses. I know this is a significant challenge in our selfie-crazed world. The lenses of comparison, judgment, lust, and anger are much easier to put on than the lenses of peace, forgiveness, compassion, and love. But you need to upgrade your perspective so you can walk fully in your purpose and experience a more profound joy by seeing others through the lens of God's love and grace.

"Be kind to one another, tenderhearted, forgiving one another, as God in Christ forgave you" (Ephesians 4:32).

Jonah 4:2-3

"And he prayed to the LORD and said, "O LORD, is not this what I said when I was yet in my country? That is why I made haste to flee to Tarshish; for I knew that you are a gracious God and merciful, slow to anger and abounding in steadfast love, and relenting from disaster. Therefore now, O LORD, please take my life from me, for it is better for me to die than to live."

In contrast with the prayer in chapter 2, which is positive and praiseful, this prayer is more hostile and defensive. This prayer focuses on Jonah, but the former focuses on God. This prayer shows Jonah's lack of appreciation. The prayer in chapter 2 shows his gratefulness.

During his prayer to the Lord, Jonah's reason for fleeing to Tarshish now becomes identified. He was afraid that the Ninevites would repent and that God would be compassionate to this ancient enemy of God's chosen nation, Israel. Jonah is claiming that he predicted God's divine forgiveness at the beginning of the story. However, the text in chapter 1 does not record Jonah saying any such thing. As a matter of fact, in chapter 1, Jonah does not say anything at all when God calls him; he just runs away.

But, how could he have known that the Ninevites would repent? The repentance of the Ninevites was an unprecedented act. Was this a self-justifying declaration by Jonah as he attempted to turn his fearful flight into an act motivated by a clear vision of the future? We may never know. However, we know that Jonah had a problem with God's level of grace. Maybe, Jonah had a problem with accepting that God's steadfast love, grace, and mercy were not limited to the nation of Israel.

Jonah felt so angry and disappointed that he asked God to take his life. From a psychological perspective, by asking the Lord to take his life, Jonah shows us that he felt emotionally lost. He felt lost because of his wounded pride, and he felt lost because he felt like he had contributed to the Israelites' impending suffering. Like Jonah, sometimes we feel we are on the right path in our own lives, and other times we feel lost, both literally and metaphorically.

Deal with Your Emotions

Emotions are a normal and vital part of your life. They are an essential part of your soul. Some of your emotions are positive such as joy, happiness, excitement, gratitude, love, and contentment. But you also have experienced emotions you did not wish to feel—negative emotions such as fear, sadness, and anger.

Do you remember the pain you experienced dwelling on undesired feelings? Understandably, you can struggle with how to deal with them effectively.

It can be enticing to act on what you are feeling in the moment, but it often doesn't fix the situation that caused the negative emotions. As a matter of fact, it may lead to more difficulties which you will have to deal with down the road. This is especially true when we feel a negative emotion too frequently, too strongly, or dwell on it for too long. Learning to manage your emotions is the key to peace of mind.

Therefore, I want to share four fundamental reasons from the Bible why you need to learn how to manage your emotions.

1. **Learn to manage your emotions because they are frequently unreliable.**

Your emotions are often incorrect and flawed. Your feelings will frequently lead you down a path that God doesn't want you to take. You cannot depend on everything you feel! Proverbs 14:12 says, ***"There is a way that seems right to a man, but its end is the way to death."***

2. **Learn to manage your emotions because you do not want to be manipulated.**

If you do not control your emotions, they will consume you, and your moods will manipulate you. And if your feelings are always controlling you, other people will take advantage of you. Proverbs 29:11 says, ***"A fool gives full vent to his spirit, but a wise man quietly holds it back."***

3. **Learn to manage your emotions because you want to please the Lord.**

The Lord cannot rule your life if your emotions are ruling your life. If you make your choices based on how you feel, you have made your feelings a god, and your feelings become an idol. Romans 8:5-8 says, ***"For those who live according to the flesh set their minds on the things of the flesh, but those who live according to the Spirit set their minds on the things of the Spirit. For to set the mind on the flesh is death, but to set the mind on the Spirit is life and peace. For the mind that is set on the flesh is hostile to God, for it does not submit to God's law; indeed, it cannot. Those who are in the flesh cannot please God."***

4. Learn to manage your emotions because you want to prosper in life.

Several studies have revealed that your emotional intelligence is critical when it comes to success. How many individuals do you know who ruined their lives because of something they did in anger or missed a great opportunity because of their lack of self-control? Proverbs 14:29 says, ***"Whoever is slow to anger has great understanding, but he who has a hasty temper exalts folly."***

It is so important not to let your emotions dictate your actions. When you decide to embrace life's challenges and trust in God, I believe you will experience a newfound sense of hope and peace, knowing He will work all things together for your good. Furthermore, when you give your heart to Jesus, that commitment includes your emotions. Jesus wants to be Lord over your thoughts, your actions, and your feelings.

Jonah 4:4

"And the LORD said, "Do you do well to be angry?"

In this verse, God's question was not an inquiry by which God seeks information concerning Jonah's emotional state. God's examination was not rebuking Jonah either. But instead, God's question was an expression of His interest in Jonah's self-centered attitude. God's question was suggesting that Jonah might not be viewing the situation correctly. God's question showed Jonah that he had a wicked aspect to his character, and he should not be angry about Nineveh being forgiven.

A key element of leading a quality life is understanding that you are part of something larger than yourself. Jonah has a difficult time with this concept, even though he could connect to a larger reality. For example, at the end of chapter 1, Jonah seems genuinely concerned about the sailors' welfare on the boat. During his prayer from the belly of the big fish, he seems to understand himself as a servant to the Most-High God.

But here, in chapter 4, Jonah falls back into his self-focused mindset. He was making everything about him and his feelings. Jonah was feeling the frustration of not understanding God's actions in the light of His character.

It's Not All About You

Nearly everything in our society—songs, video games, TV shows, news stories, and advertisements—says you have to think about yourself first. But the more you lead a self-focused life, the more you are susceptible to discouragement and frustration.

Every time you forget that it is not all about you, you will become prideful, fearful, hostile, and jealous. Those feelings will always lead you down a painful path because they keep you focused on yourself. The Bible says in James 3:16, ***"For where jealousy and selfish ambition exist, there will be disorder and every vile practice."***

You need to understand that life is not all about you! God put you on this earth to glorify Him. He has a message He wants you to declare to others, and that message is not about you. It's about Jesus Christ and His kingdom! 2 Corinthians 4:5 says, ***"In their case the god of this world has blinded the minds of the unbelievers, to keep them from seeing the light of the gospel of the glory of Christ, who is the image of God. For what we proclaim is not ourselves, but Jesus Christ as Lord, with ourselves as your servants for Jesus' sake."***

God is not only interested in what you are doing, but He is also interested in why you are doing what you are doing. He cares about the motivations of your heart and mind. Why you are doing something always determines how long you will be doing it. If you are motivated by self-seeking ambition, that will never be good enough. You will eventually get frustrated and quit.

However, when you are motivated to do something because of how it advances the Kingdom of God and glorifies King Jesus, you will have the inspiration you need to see it through.

God is counting on you to let your light shine through the dark places. If you have gone through a level of discomfort and pain, He wants you to help other people going through that same hurt and pain. He wants you to share your wisdom and insight. In other words, what you have been through will help somebody else get through it. God can use the problems in your life to give you a ministry to others.

Your actions motivate others to dream more, learn more, do more, and grow to be more. You are a leader in your community. So, be on the lookout for others you can encourage and lead by example with your actions. People would rather witness a testimony than listen to one any day. They would rather you walk with them than merely tell the way.

"Let each of you look not only to his own interests, but also to the interests of others" (Philippians 2:4).

Lessons from the Lord

Jonah 4:5

"Jonah went out of the city and sat to the east of the city and made a booth for himself there. He sat under it in the shade, till he should see what would become of the city."

First question: Why does this verse begin with the words "Jonah went out"? Of course, Jonah left Nineveh immediately after issuing his proclamation.

In verse 5, the text returns to the earlier moment in the story when Jonah proclaims that Nineveh will be overturned in 40 days (Jonah 3:4). The sequence of the verses in this chapter does not follow the series of events as they unfolded. The conversation between God and Jonah described in this chapter, verses 1-4, took place after Jonah departed from Nineveh, depicted here in verse 5.

There is no separate past perfect form in Hebrew to describe an action that has already been completed. Verbs in the regular past tense form are used for this purpose. Therefore, ideally, this verse should begin, "Now Jonah had went out of the city and sat to the east of the city and made a booth for himself there."

Second question: Why did Jonah construct shelter and sit down to watch what would happen to Nineveh? Did Jonah think that judgment might fall on Nineveh, or was he waiting for God to explain His actions? Perhaps he expected that the Ninevites' repentance would vanish swiftly and that God would then call him to pronounce the judgment that he so wanted to see.

Understanding that verses 1-4 took place after verse 5, we can recognize that Jonah did not know if the Ninevites' repentance would be sufficient to postpone God's judgment. Therefore, he dwelled somewhere on the mountains' slopes that rise to the east of Nineveh to gain a good view of whatever might happen. When he realized God's mercy on Nineveh, he became displeased and angry (Jonah 4:1).

Jonah 4:6

"Now the LORD God appointed a plant and made it come up over Jonah, that it might be a shade over his head, to save him from his discomfort. So Jonah was exceedingly glad because of the plant."

Notice the shift in the name of God. The beginning of the verse is one of the rare appearances of the compound name "Lord God" in scripture. The Hebrew translation of the name shift is "Elohim Yahweh" (Lord God). "Elohim" is used in scripture when emphasizing God's might, His creative power, and His attributes of justice and rulership.

With His authority and might, God ministered tenderly to Jonah and continued to manifest compassion for him by providing a shaded plant that relieved the discomfort of the blistering Mesopotamian sun. It is impossible to identify the exact plant that God provided. This detail is similar to the species of the big fish. None of these specifics are known, and none of them are essential. The fish is some giant species big enough to swallow a person, and the plant must be leafy enough to provide significant shade. Knowing the precise type of plant would not add to our understanding of the events of the story.

Furthermore, it is possible that because Jonah was in the belly of the fish for three days, the skin of his flesh was tender and sensitive to the touch causing him not to be able to withstand the sun's heat. This thought explains why Jonah required additional protection from the sun.

Note: The climate of Mesopotamia is haphazard. Summer's temperatures range from 110 to 130 degrees Fahrenheit. Eight months out of the year are dry, and the remaining months are a rainy and snowy season.

This verse concludes by describing Jonah's reaction to the plant. He was "exceedingly glad." This is the only time that we read that Jonah was glad, and it was because he was physically comfortable.

The word "discomfort" is translated from the Hebrew word *"ra'ah."* Ra'ah is the same Hebrew word translated to "evil" where it describes the Ninevites' evil (Jonah 1:2, 3:8). The word "displeased," where it expresses Jonah's displeasure over God's decision to spare the city (verse 1), is also the Hebrew word *"ra'ah."* Jonah's attitudes were as evil in God's sight as the Ninevites' actions.

Even though God viewed Jonah's attitude as evil, the Lord provided a plant to protect him and to teach Jonah to be concerned with life beyond himself. Now, I have a question for you. Are you concerned with life beyond yourself?

Beyond Your Benefits

Jonah reminds me of the people I regularly encounter who think only of themselves. Individuals who act as if the whole world exists for their benefit. Under no circumstances should you ever fall for the seductive attraction of self-centeredness. Your life develops much more when you see yourself as part of a larger community. In other words, you should avoid seeing yourself as a solo artist but view yourself as being a part of a large orchestra. In fact,

You did not choose God. God chose you so that you could go among your community and bear fruit.

Let's imagine that you play the violin. Sometimes the whole orchestra plays. Sometimes it is just the violins, violas, and the cello that plays. Sometimes the horns play, and you sit quietly. And every once in a while, you have a solo part. In other words, you do not stand at the center of the world; you are a tiny part of a much larger whole.

You live out this truth when you help people rebuild the ruins of their lives. God wants to use you to bring boundless hope and peace to people worldwide who are desperately searching for truth and light. Your outreach is critical, and when you work with others, you are replacing their fear with your love and faith.

The Bible says you are an ambassador for Christ (2 Corinthians 5:20), speaking on behalf of King Jesus. When you tell others about the good news of Jesus Christ, God is making His appeal through you. You are a vessel for the Kingdom of God. Your faith can help grow the faith of others as you share God's Word with them.

Let's take this one step further. Let's look at two passages. The first passage says:

And he said to him, You shall love the Lord your God with all your heart and with all your soul and with all your mind. This is the great and first commandment. And a second is like it: You shall love your neighbor as yourself (Matthew 22:37-39).

Did you notice Jesus saying to love God with all your heart, soul, and mind? That is called worship! Then Jesus continued by saying, love your neighbor as yourself. That is called service!

Now, let's take a look at a second passage:

And Jesus came and said to them, All authority in heaven and on earth has been given to me. Go therefore and make disciples of all nations, baptizing them in the name of the Father and of the Son and of the Holy Spirit, teaching them to observe all that I have commanded you. And behold, I am with you always, to the end of the age (Matthew 28:18-20).

You will notice Jesus said, make disciples. That is called fellowship! He continued by saying, baptize them in the name of the Father, Son, and Holy Spirit. That is called sanctification! Lastly, Jesus said, teach them to do everything I've commanded you. That is called discipleship!

So, what does all of this means? It means you are needed! You are needed in your local church. You are needed in your community. You are needed in this world.

You were created to share your life with others! You are alive to contribute with your life. You and I are not just believers; we are belongers.

Jonah 4:7-8

"But when dawn came up the next day, God appointed a worm that attacked the plant, so that it withered. When the sun rose, God appointed a scorching east wind, and the sun beat down on the head of Jonah so that he was faint. And he asked that he might die and said, "It is better for me to die than to live."

The stress on God's sovereignty continues. God provided a storm, a fish, a plant, a worm, and the wind to fulfill His purpose. Clearly, God was manipulating Jonah's circumstances to teach him some valuable lessons.

Many scholars believe that the scorching east wind that God provided was a sirocco. A sirocco is a Mediterranean wind that comes from the Sahara and reaches hurricane speeds. A sirocco causes dusty dry conditions along the northern coast of Africa, storms in the Mediterranean Sea, and chilly, wet weather in Europe. The duration of a sirocco may be as short as half a day or may last several days.

Sirocco winds with speeds of up to 65 miles per hour are most common during the autumn and the spring. They reach a peak in March, and in November when it is very hot. If scorching east winds was a sirocco or something similar, then the preceding description helps us appreciate why it had such a miserable effect on Jonah.

Jonah's soul (mind, emotions, and willpower) was exhausted. He became quite tormented to the extent that he could no longer stand on his own because of the heat. His situation and circumstance consumed him; therefore, he preferred death over life.

Faith through Difficulties

Have you ever had days when everything seems to go wrong? Of course, you have! Difficulties and challenges are the bullies that step into your path and try to wrestle you to the ground and pin you until you cry. The voices of your difficulties and challenges will try to outshout both God and your own thoughts until you are confused. They will appear so large that you can only see what's right in front of you — the problems, the obstacles, the burdens, and the stresses.

But did you know that the Bible says we should not be surprised by life's problems?

Having faith in the Lord during difficult times can be extremely hard. Agonizing. Even physically painful. However, I want to testify that trusting Jesus in challenging times (even finding joy through trials) is possible for any of us.

1 Peter 1:6-7 says, ***"In this you rejoice, though now for a little while, if necessary, you have been grieved by various trials, so that the tested genuineness of your faith—more precious than gold that perishes though it is tested by fire—may be found to result in praise and glory and honor at the revelation of Jesus Christ."***

When your world is falling apart, it is easy to focus on the pain, the problems, the pressure, and the difficulties. It is a natural response. But the godly response is to repent (return to your true essence) and focus on God's love and grace.

If you believe in Jesus as the Christ, you need to understand that nothing comes into your life by accident. Everything is God-filtered. The Bible doesn't say everything is good, but everything will work together for your good.

Romans 8:28 says, ***"And we know that for those who love God all things work together for good, for those who are called according to his purpose."*** This scripture teaches you that your difficulties, frustrations, disruptions, and trials will all serve a purpose.

The problem we have is understanding how the issues and complications work together for our good. We struggle to see how our problems have a greater purpose. But God uses our difficulties to prove our faith.

So how does God want you to respond to difficulties? James 1:2-3 says, ***"Count it all joy, my brothers, when you meet trials of various kinds, for you know that the testing of your faith produces steadfastness."***

The Lord uses difficulties to test your faith and to increase your faith. When you worship and rejoice continually, remain grateful and positive, and keep an encouraging attitude despite things not going right, your faith is stretched and strengthened.

In the difficult times, God has promised that you are going to overflow with abundance. You are not going to lack anything you need. There will be plenty of strength, plenty of healing, plenty of peace, and plenty of grace. You cannot become who you were created to be without going through winds of testing.

How you respond in these difficult times will determine whether you come out bitter or if you come out better.

Jonah 4:9

"But God said to Jonah, "Do you do well to be angry for the plant?" And he said, "Yes, I do well to be angry, angry enough to die."

In verse 9, the text uses the same word, angry, from Jonah 4:4 to describe Jonah's sense of loss over the death of the plant. However, unlike verse 4, God responds to Jonah differently. This time, God rebukes him with a question and retort, and Jonah asserts that he has a right to be angry enough to want to die.

Jonah's anger about the withered plant was selfish based on his own comfort, for he genuinely did not care about the plant. Also, he was not actually concerned about life and death in general. He was only concerned about his personal comfort. At this point, Jonah had become utterly indifferent to the fate of the Ninevites.

When Jonah recited his prayer from the belly of the big fish, he seemed to be changing from being self-centered to appreciating his situation in the context of the larger world. He appeared to have learned from his mistake and was maturing spiritually in the story. He certainly seemed to be deeply concerned about his relationship with God. But now, as we approach the story's conclusion, Jonah seems to have reverted to his earlier self-centeredness. Despite his experience in the belly of the fish, Jonah has not grown spiritually. And spiritual growth is an essential key to a purposeful and fulfilled life.

Grow Up Spiritually

We all need to understand that growing up is a process, both physically and spiritually. We must allow God to develop that process in us. You didn't become a full-grown human overnight. And you don't become a full-grown Christian overnight.

Nonetheless, I would like to ask you a question. After you experience a difficult challenge, do you learn from it? Furthermore, do you know that it's not the Father's will for you to remain a child spiritually but to grow up and become mature in Him through your faith in Jesus Christ?

God created you and wants you to become more like His anointed one, King Jesus. He wants you to grow up spiritually, conforming us to His image! The Bible says in Ephesians 4:15, ***"Rather, speaking the truth in love, we are to grow up in every way into him who is the head, into Christ."*** Also, Romans 8:29 says, ***"For those whom he foreknew he also predestined to be conformed to the image of his Son, in***

order that he might be the firstborn among many brothers."

As a minister, I'm always asked, "Why is this happening to me?" Let me tell you why:

The good, the bad, the unpleasant, the stuff you bring on yourself, and the stuff other people do to you, help you grow spiritually. God is not the author of wickedness, but sometimes, God allows bad things to happen so your faith can be strengthened, and you can mature, develop, and change.

Therefore, rather than asking God, "Why is this happening to me?" you should ask God, "What do you want me to learn from this?" You should ask God, "How does this help me become more like Christ?"

Every problem has the potential to cause physical, moral, and spiritual pitfalls. But as you climb your way up out of the pit, you can gain proper perspective and understand how those low moments were exactly what you needed to bring you to your Promised Land.

God teaches you love, by placing you around hateful and unloving people. He teaches you true joy and contentment as you recover from grief and loss. The Lord teaches how to be peaceful in the middle of chaos and confusion. He teaches you patience in those long, snaking, boring lines at theme parks. God teaches you kindness, gentleness, and self-control by allowing you to work with disrespectful coworkers.

God will teach you all of these qualities throughout your life, which will take the rest of your life. It's a process. It's a journey. The Lord, our God, will use all kinds of situations and problems in your life to help you grow spiritually and become more like Christ.

Jonah 4:10-11

"And the LORD said, "You pity the plant, for which you did not labor, nor did you make it grow, which came into being in a night and perished in a night. And should not I pity Nineveh, that great city, in which there are more than 120,000 persons who do not know their right hand from their left, and also much cattle?"

The Lord points out that Jonah cared deeply about a plant, over which he had not labored and which he had not nurtured. After all, it had appeared overnight and died overnight. The word "perished" recalls the desperate hope of the captain (1:6) and the king (3:9) that their people not perish. Jonah cares deeply about the death of one plant because its death reduced his own comfort level.

God teaches Jonah that even though he took pity on the plant, He takes pity on Nineveh because of His glory. God explains that He takes pity on all of His creations. He would like Jonah to see that all people have value. However, Jonah seems only interested in himself.

Commentators and scholars have carefully looked at the description of the Ninevites in verse 11. Ibn Ezra does not take the number 120,000 to be the population of Nineveh or the number of people who had repented for their sins. But instead, the number of individuals who had not sinned, including children. Rabbi Kimchi teaches the number 120,000 should not mistakenly be taken to refer to the number of men in Nineveh. It includes men and women that did not know how to escape their troubles.

The expression "do not know the difference between their right and left hand" is a denoting expression that means lacking in knowledge and innocent to a certain degree. Not being able to distinguish between the right and left is a sign of divine and spiritual infancy. God teaches Jonah that Nineveh has a shallow understanding of truth and needs someone to teach them the elementary truths of God's sovereignty.

We see this same lesson of God's sovereignty being taught to the Southern Kingdom of Judah through Amos' prophecy. The Bible says in Amos 9: 11-12, ***"In that day I will raise up the booth of David that is fallen and repair its breaches, and raise up its ruins and rebuild it as in the days of old, that they may possess the remnant of Edom and all the nations who are called by my name, declares the Lord who does this."*** Then we see the fulfillment of this prophecy through the Apostle Peter in Acts 10 and the explanation of the prophecy in Acts 15.

The final question the Lord asks to conclude the book is the absolute highlight of God's lesson to the prophet and the nation of Israel. And that lesson is that no one is beyond the reach of God's hand. His benevolence and mercy await anyone if they only repent full-heartedly.

Note: Jonah and Nahum are the only two books in the Bible that end with questions, and they both have to do with Nineveh.

Final Thoughts

The book of Jonah shows a prophet of God doing what many Christians are now doing actively today; not forgiving and being unwilling to share the gospel with people who are different mentally, physically, and socially. Like Nineveh, our communities inhabit very sinful and confused individuals. Crowded graveyards and overfull prisons bear dramatic proof to the fact that sin runs rampant in our society every day. Child abuse, domestic and foreign terrorism, and repressive governments, the world seems to be overflowing with violence, hatred, and corruption.

Reading, seeing, and hearing about the wickedness of people, and perhaps experiencing it personally, we find ourselves wishing for revenge upon the culprits. We understand and recognize the necessity of God's authority and forgiveness; however, sometimes, we might prefer a judgment to come upon those wicked individuals rather than grace.

We'd rather entertain the idea of God's judgment because we feel like it is what some individuals deserve, and they are beyond redemption. We wish they would be wiped out of our future because, like Jonah, we recognize the threat they have on our communities and families.

If we are honest with ourselves, we have a hard time forgiving people who hurt us or hurt others. But what if, during your hurt, frustration, and pain, the Lord tells you to take a message of forgiveness and love through Jesus Christ to those who offended you or even tried to destroy you and your family? How would you respond? What would you do? Would you do what God told you to do?

It is easy for us to read about the story of Jonah and chastise him. But if we are put in the same dilemma, many of us would make the same decision Jonah made. We wouldn't want God to pour out His grace on a society or a group of wicked and violent people, like Nineveh, especially if their wickedness impacts our lives on a personal level. But here is the truth: **God will forgive people we believe do not deserve forgiveness, and we can't do anything about it!**

Can I ask you a couple of questions? Does Nineveh remind you of someone? Maybe someone in your community or someone in your family. Perhaps it's your parents or a former best friend. Would you react like Jonah, be disobedient, and try to run away from your assignment, or are you bold enough to be graceful and forgive, standing in your authority in Christ?

Running from your purpose, calling, or divine assignment will cause you more problems and a significant amount of agony. The truth is, there is no running from God. You cannot hide from the Lord. He is omnipresent, which means, He is everywhere at the same time. There is no place you can go where God cannot see you, and there are no thoughts or feelings that you can hide from Him.

Despite all your objections and procrastination, what the Lord wishes to achieve through you will come to pass. God loves you too much to let you miss your destiny or your divine assignment. However, the more you ignore God, the harder your heart becomes, the harder it is for you to hear God's voice calling you, which will make your life's journey more difficult. The Bible warns us in Ephesians 4:18, ***"They are darkened in their understanding, alienated from the life of God because of the ignorance that is in them, due to their hardness of heart."***

God's love and grace are manifested in His accessibility to all, regardless of our name, reputation, status, nationality, or race. We are called, as Christians, to help others to pursue His presence. We are tasked to help people run to God's open arms. We're called to help those individuals who have hurt us or disagree with us.

How much more comfortable would life be if you, unlike Jonah, would submit to God without delay? How much more peace will you have if you love others as much as you love yourself? How much more favor will you have if you are obedient to the Lord's instructions? Did you know you can bring pleasure to the Lord through obedience? Any act of obedience is also an act of worship.

Obedience may not always seem like the fun option, but it is always worth it because souls are connected to your life. Meaning, your obedience to the Lord will lead to great favor and blessings while opening the doors of salvation and redemption for others. In other words, do not be afraid to be obedient because you will obtain His promises when you obey Him. Please understand, it is not just about you, your family, or your pain. It is about advancing the Kingdom of God for the glory of God.

So, instead of running or hiding from the Lord, run to Him and lay open everything in your life and heart. Take comfort in the fact that He knows everything about you, and He is there for you.

Now, let us pray:

Heavenly Father, what a comfort to understand that Your mercy, grace, and love toward us will never change or fade because it is not based on who we are, but on who You are! Help us remember You are in charge of our lives. Help us trust your way and live out Your perfect will for our lives every single day! Give us the discernment to know Your will and obey the commands You give us. Help us remember there is no place where we can hide from You.

Lord, we want You to be our first option when the storms come. Let us be a light for those who are in the middle of the sea without hope and help them arrive to the safe port we have in You.

It is in the name of Jesus, the Christ; we pray, Amen!

Can You Do Me A Favor?

First, if you enjoyed *The Book of Jonah*, would you take a few moments to write a review? Leaving a short review will help me out massively and would be much appreciated.

Secondly, please send a copy of this book if you know someone who needs to be encouraged, inspired, and motivated.

Thirdly, remember, there are blessings that await you when you choose to take a step of faith and move forward! If you are having trouble taking that step forward, please allow me to pray for you. Send me a prayer request so my team and I can join you in prayer: **tonywarrick.com/prayerrequest/**

Lastly, don't forget to subscribe to my website and catch all my new releases, daily devotionals, and monthly newsletter. You can sign up here: **tonywarrick.com**

Thank you so much for reading The Book of Jonah!

About the Author

Dr. Tony L. Warrick has always had a passion for transformation. This passion unveiled his purpose to see people be all that God has created them to be by connecting the transforming power of Jesus Christ to everyday living.

Born and raised in Washington, D.C., Dr. Warrick overcame incredible odds from his youth by pulling from the grace he experienced during his darkest lessons to help individuals change their lives through spiritual health, personal growth, and professional development. His writings provide daily action steps for every area of a Christian life. It is his aspiration that people are equipped with practical principles to navigate the complex challenges life can bring while moving forward and making a significant impact in their community.

To learn more about Dr. Warrick, please visit:

TonyWarrick.com

twitter.com/IamTonyWarrick

facebook.com/IamTonyWarrick

linkedin.com/in/iamtonywarrick

instagram.com/iamtonywarrick

www.ingramcontent.com/pod-product-compliance
Lightning Source LLC
Chambersburg PA
CBHW071857020426
42331CB00010B/2557

* 9 7 8 1 9 5 5 2 5 3 0 1 7 *